Storefront Day Care Centers

Storefront Day Care Centers

The Radical Berlin Experiment

edited by an Authors' Collective

translated by Catherine Lord and
Renée Neu Watkins

Beacon Press   Boston

German text: © 1970 by Verlag Kiepenheuer & Witsch, Cologne
English translation: © 1973 by Beacon Press
Storefront Day Care Centers was first published under the title
Berliner Kinderläden by Verlag Kiepenheuer & Witsch, Cologne.
Beacon Press books are published under the auspices
of the Unitarian Universalist Association
Simultaneous publication in Canada by Saunders of Toronto, Ltd.
All rights reserved
Printed in the United States of America

9   8   7   6   5   4   3   2   1

Library of Congress Cataloging in Publication

Main entry under title:
Storefront day care centers.
   Translation of Berliner Kinderläden.
      1. Day nurseries — Berlin.   2. Education, Preschool.
   I. Lord, Catherine, trans.   II. Watkins, Renée Neu, trans.

HV861.G32B47713   362.7'1   72–75544
ISBN 0–8070–3168–2

Contents

Preface

Storefront Day Care Centers — The Radical Berlin Experiment

The unwieldy but literal translation would have been "The Storefront Day Care Centers of Berlin — Nonauthoritarian Education and the Socialist Struggle." To those who equate educational experiments with an enlightened permissiveness, the book would seem to be handicapped from the start by a hopeless contradiction between freedom for the individual and the collective discipline required by a militant socialism. But the Student Federation of Social Democrats (SDS) parents who founded the centers did not want another Summerhill. They didn't want to produce contented souls — be they university professors, hairdressers, or garage mechanics; they wanted revolutionaries. This meant permissiveness to free the children from those "normal" family pressures which breed people resigned to the system, trapped in passivity, exploitativeness, or ineffectual rebellion.

Permissiveness, but not in an isolated haven, because these parents wanted their children to grow up to be capable of both judging what social changes were necessary and working systematically with others to achieve them. Since they thought that the family covertly brainwashes children anyway, they decided on an openly political education. It wasn't a matter of methodical indoctrination, instilling reverence for symbols and slogans. They simply explained to the children how they, as Marxists, saw Berlin. They talked about landlords and tenants, the demonstrations they marched in, the policeman on the block.

There's no avoiding the fact that in this book about kindergartens, remarkably little is said about people. Unlike Kozol or Herndon or Dennison, the authors do not portray individual character and experience. There are only occasional glimpses: the harassed teacher forcing herself to intervene no more than necessary in the feuds of milk-spitting, pencil-stabbing little children. The book is closer, perhaps, to the work of Frantz Fanon in conveying the feel of acting with political intentions. It is an ideological analysis of the growth of a movement, a description of ideas being tested and changed. We see people as part of an ongoing movement — their concern with finding the right theories, their belief that acting on the right theories will bring the right results, their effort to analyze events consistently, their inevitable quarrels, their honesty about admitting failures and mistakes. Since the authors have included various documents (political speeches, magazine articles, government reports, SDS pamphlets), we can follow the movement in the wider context of left wing politics, and of public opinion as shaped by the mass media and officialdom.

The centers, started by women's liberation members who were tired of being excluded from political activities due to the lack of day care facilities, became SDS's major concrete accomplishment, directly involving at least a hundred women and influencing many others. As soon as other SDS members realized the importance of the centers, the women had to cope with male volunteers who acted as if the centers were their invention and slipped into the old habit of trying to run the show. Although the women wanted to work with men (two women and a man wrote this book), they had to fight hard to keep their power. Their delegate to the SDS convention in 1968 voices the women's fury at being elbowed aside and explains that much more is involved than a histrionic power struggle, for the women's liberation groups and the male members of SDS have very different plans for the future of the centers.

Initially, the government thought the centers were harmless and raved about these new parent-run programs as models of the "civic functioning of the family." The Berlin Senate had been harshly criticized by the press for doing nothing about the shortage of day care facilities and, as the authors suggest, the Senate welcomed the centers so noisily and enthusiastically to divert public attention from the fact that the original problem remained unalleviated.

Then party politics closed in. The press set off a scandal by pointing out that the government was giving money to institutions favoring extreme permissiveness and Communist teachings. It became obvious that those who ran the centers were not trying to save the family but to destroy it. The liberal press made the centers appear chaotic and orgiastic, thoroughly filthy; the right wing sensationalist papers complained that the government was tolerating "Commie" schools where children played such games as killing Americans in Vietnam. Infuriated by the slanders of one magazine in particular, the liberal *Der Stern*, some of the parents marched their children down to the editorial offices, where the nervous staff watched the group spray-paint the walls and slash upholstery. *Stern* coyly assumed an air of wounded gentility in its article about the incident. Thus, although the courts had stopped distribution of the libelous issue of *Stern*, the public was left with the impression of innocent journalists besieged by irrational subversives. In response to the inquiries of outraged Senators, the government spewed forth a mass of official non-sense-prose and found ways to cut off funds for the centers.

The authors, as Marxists, point out that in capitalist society there is a basic contradiction between the material abundance produced by an elaborate system of social cooperation and the poverty created by the monopolization of wealth. This means that the masses are educated (and fed and housed and entertained) only to the degree and in the manner which will keep them docile, available, and cheap. Over and over again, the authors insist that an educational system cannot be truly changed unless this fundamental contradiction of capitalism is eliminated by the creation of a society in which the resources and means of production are democratically controlled. Fragmentary reforms cannot work; only revolution can make a real difference. Simply by the power of repetition, one is forced to come to terms with the implication that attempts at change in any sphere should be evaluated on the basis of the damage they do to the network which permits society to function for the profit of the few.

Clearly, the more radical people in the centers went on the assumption that a change in early childhood education would threaten the capitalist system. Children raised in peer groups, open about their instinctual needs and accustomed to making collective decisions, would grow up to respect human rights and challenge exploitation. But the centers as they were could be accepted only by the middle class intelligentsia. Could they be adapted to suit the needs of the working class? The movement split on this issue.

The liberals continued to run essentially elitist nonauthoritarian centers; others turned to working class districts where, although the desperate need for day care facilities favored them from the start, parents didn't have time to run the same kind of centers. The radical parents moved in two directions: some wanted to organize workers around getting day care facilities from unions or factories or government; others, seeing that working class mothers who were aware of their oppression tended to think radical education was a circuitous way to improve their lives, joined existing workers' organizations to press for economic and political advantages.

The Day Care Center movement should not be judged a failure because of this fragmentation. Never, of course, was there unanimous agreement on how to use the centers as a tool for change, but some semblance of unity was necessary when negotiations with the government were in progress. When political differences finally became open, the radical group chose to try to reach the working class even though they knew how thoroughly it had been integrated into the system — convinced of its own powerlessness, seduced by the admittedly slim chance of escape as an individual, or drugged by its distinctly restricted participation in the industrial "high standard of living." But organizing in working class districts is not as flamboyant an activity as running free schools for middle class children and is not likely to attract similar publicity. Still, opening new choices to workers may prove to be another step up the mountain.

Catherine Lord

Renée Neu Watkins

Introduction

The Storefront Day Care Centers offered, for the first time, a practical alternative to the child rearing practices that prevailed in the West German Republic.

The centers agreed on the principle of nonauthoritarian or non-repressive education. These terms clearly assume an opposition to the methods and aims of the traditional authoritarian system of child rearing. But one cannot merely pass along a system of anti-authoritarian educational techniques which can be followed like a recipe; the first step must be an examination and criticism of authoritarian child rearing methods.

Education or child rearing involves confronting a child, in every stage of his development, with the conditions under which people live and the attitudes they hold in a given society. Individuals and institutions concerned with child care provide education either by aiming for explicit educational ends or simply by transmitting their own styles of behavior and their own values. The goal is to make children into competent and useful members of the existing society. This is the process of socialization; in its first phase, which ends around age six in our society, the foundations are laid in the individual for the kinds of development open to him later. Forms of socialization vary greatly among cultures.

Before the beginning of this century, when Sigmund Freud discovered the significance of infantile sexuality, no one took the first phase of socialization seriously; the child was considered simply an unfinished adult. As a result of his discovery, thorough research was done to establish the natural stages of child development, to define the influence of environment, and to evaluate the long-run effects of different methods of child rearing.

For several decades, anthropologists have been studying the variety of child rearing practices, especially in so-called primitive societies. A comparison of these practices is the easiest way to grasp the impact of early childhood training. Different forms of socialization create different types of social character. People in highly industrialized, "civilized" societies generally differ from

those in other societies in degree of aggressiveness, ego-centered-
ness, capacity for love, intelligence, etc. Different socioeconomic
structures, because they necessitate particular forms of socialization, account for these variations. The family is the most significant
element in the process of socialization. For example, in his article,
"Fundamental Questions of Trans-cultural Psychiatry," Erich
Wulff compares the extended Vietnamese family with the nuclear
family of bourgeois capitalist society and explains why the kind
of ego disturbances characteristic of our society cannot be found
among the Vietnamese:

The extended and the nuclear family derive from the requirements of different ecomomic systems. In small communities engaged in technologically primitive rice cultivation, extended
families and close ties among neighbors are an absolute economic
necessity. Under such conditions, irrigation and dike building
projects cannot possibly be achieved except by collective work.
This is not, of course, the only cause for the existence of the social
institutions of the extended family and the village community,
but it is probably the most important one. Another reason lies in
the total absence of any provision by the wider society for hunger,
illness, old age, and natural disasters: the community is the only
source of protection. Although the group of grandparents, uncles,
aunts, nephews, cousins, and the many siblings in a house may be
only partially involved in agricultural production, they are nur-
tured and supported along with the others; these relatively weak
members of the group form a reservoir of manpower for child care
and rearing. They perform this task in cyclical alternation with the
parents, by filling in when they are working. This is no paper
construct. The fact is, for example in Vietnam, that those family
members, especially the older children, unsuited for much of the
labor of rice cultivation, actively participate in the care and training of small children, sometimes during the very first year of
infancy, and almost always during the second year. This situation
offers children "multilateral" possibilities for identification. The
resultant formation of a collective group ego rather than an individual ego awareness thus derives from the family structure required by a specific agrarian mode of production.
    In the extended family, the fact that someone is always available
to care for the children has another important consequence for
the process of socialization. It makes possible a much later weaning and dissolution of the almost symbiotic physical relationship

between mother and child than that financially feasible for the nuclear family of an industrial worker or even a white collar worker. In such a family, either both parents work or, while the father and older children work, the mother is fully occupied by the tasks of housework. The effort to preserve most of the parents' and older children's time, both for work and for the recreation and rest needed to maintain the capacity to work, requires a rigid feeding schedule, early weaning from the breast and from physical symbiosis with the mother, as well as premature toilet training, accompanied by punishment or threats of the withdrawal of love. The results include societally typical oral and anal deprivations, tailored almost exclusively to the parents' need for rest, rather than to the learning processes of children. Naturally, there are striking class differences in this regard. In the case of a very wealthy family, with servants, nurses, and perhaps governesses, there may be, insofar as the educational ideology of the class permits, a marked modification of the strictness of child rearing practices during the oral and anal phases. Shifting the burden of work to dependents also gives the children more "inner freedom" and greater "magnanimity" of character. But where such a transference of duties is impossible, the rule is either strict regimentation or, the other side of the coin, neglect — often both in rapid alternation.

However, the structure of social institutions and their concomitant role expectations is not a historical accident, for they depend upon the prevailing economic system. Every economic system, shaped by the state of the forces of production as well as by the production and property relationships, sets, for each class, the average measure of socially useful work and allocates it among the sexes, age groups, etc. These economic demands affect not only work life, but the entire sphere of social life, including the so-called private sector — family life, leisure, educational practices, etc. The structures created in the world of work by any given mode of production form, in a sense, the negative image of the society's private life, which encompasses the socialization processes. For instance, if work time fixes the individual's leisure hours, then the demands of work also dictate which member of the family will spend what periods of time at home and will be able to attend to the children. The rhythm of work yields something like a rhythm of socialization. The economic system, however, also shapes the family structure to suit the purposes of production, and determines the requisite sex roles. And finally,

it sets the degree to which different classes and different family members utilize the products of the economy.
                                        — Erich Wulff, *Das Argument* No. 50/3, pp. 252 f.

Applying Wulff's argument, one can perhaps characterize the typical child rearing methods of the small bourgeois family as follows:

> Strong emotional ties to the parents, the only available objects for identification
>
> Early weaning
>
> Strict and early toilet training
>
> Denial and repression of infantile sexuality
>
> Small play space, due to housing conditions and the parents' need for rest
>
> Infrequent contact with peers
>
> An individualized life, which encourages egoism, property strivings accompanied by dependency, and lack of development of social skills
>
> Repression of infantile needs, which retards the development of social skills and the growth of intelligence

The means of socialization are fear, punishment (still, in our society, primarily physical blows), and the image of parents as beings against whom criticism is forbidden. Every point, however, varies with social class.

This is a valid description of the customary type of child rearing, despite the existence of an institution which partially removes children from the "natural" parental influence. For three factors determine the manner in which kindergartens function among us: only a fraction (¼) of children are exposed to them; they are primarily custodial facilities, because child rearing is intended to remain the family's prerogative; the conditions in kindergartens (large groups, little money, lack of arrangements suited to children, and trained teachers) repress infantile needs even more severely than conditions at home.

Given our society's wealth and its technological and research capacities, this type of education for small children is irresponsible and irrational. For inevitably, it leads to irresolvable conflicts in the environment, where both professional and private life are ever more depersonalized by an inescapable technology and psychological regimentation. The outcome is an increasing number of physiological and psychological illnesses and deformations.

Education in the nuclear family produces, above all, an authoritarian character, the type of basically antidemocratic citizen characteristic of our society. Adorno, among others, has demonstrated the strong tendency of the authoritarian character to favor fascist developments (*The Authoritarian Personality*, Norton, New York, 1950).

Each state evolves the system of child rearing most suited to preserve its existence. If one wants to change the educational practices, one must struggle against the socioeconomic basis of the social system.

Political education, consciously attacking the foundation and the aims of authoritarian education, must therefore confront the repressive actions of the ruling forces. The means of repression as exemplified in the case of the Storefront Day Care Centers are (1) defamation in the bourgeois mass media; (2) lack of material support for the new forms of education, or support only at the price of integration and control by the state administration; and (3) attempts to employ legal pressures against the projects and, in that way, to destroy them.

The next stage involves toleration of the new form as an experiment that can be terminated and, simultaneously, the integration of the new methods through selective reform of the traditional educational system.

Nonauthoritarian Education as Practiced in the Movement

Early in 1968, the first Storefront Day Care Centers in West Berlin were organized. The initiative came from the Action Council of Women's Liberation, founded in January by SDS. In the summer of 1968, the groups which had already formed, united in a Central Council of Socialist Day Care Centers. They defined their political task as follows: "The Central Council understands its own function as part of the socialist movement. Its future task will be to move from the self-help organization within the movement towards initiation of self-help organizations among the working masses" (Introduction to Vera Schmidt, *Three Essays*, published by the Central Council, February 1969). At the beginning of 1969 a larger public began to show interest in the Day Care Centers. At first the nonauthoritarian methods were much attacked and libelled, mainly because of their political goals. The financial support originally granted by the Senate of West Berlin to these "models of innovation in the politics of the family" was revoked.

Meanwhile, other APO groups (Ausser-Parlamentarische Opposition — extra-parliamentary opposition) began to work in the educational area. In West Berlin and the Federal Republic, various school teachers, kindergarten teachers, and social workers attempted to apply the principles of nonauthoritarian education in the institutions where they worked.

A third domain was found where the new techniques could be used and tested. This consisted mainly of children in homes and orphanages, and juvenile delinquents in reform schools and on parole. In spite of frequent institutional opposition, students and social workers struggled to work with these groups.

The various kinds of application were rather separated in practice and were usually guided by differing ideas. The kindergarten teachers in West Berlin organized a work group within a left wing gathering called the Republican Club. The social workers formed a Workshop of Critical Social Workers (AKS) and the teachers formed the Socialist Teachers' League (SLE). High points of the struggle within existing institutions were the strike of the West Berlin kindergarten teachers in the summer of 1969, and that fall, the strike of the Kreuzberg kindergarten teachers, when school was actually in progress.

The social workers and teachers initiated, with varying degrees of success, attempts to politicize (through workshops, teach-ins, go-ins, and demonstrations) the high schools and various segments of the general population. Thus sexual enlightenment (e.g., campaigns for free distribution of the Pill) was brought to youth detention centers, schools, and camps.

For socially marginal youth groups, one political high point was the exposure of extreme abuses in Tegel, the West Berlin reform school, which led to an investigation by a legislative committee and involved a series of revolts by the inmates. The agitation in West Berlin foundling homes was partially responsible for those homes being half-emptied, while student housing and communes overflowed with runaway juveniles.

The summer of 1969 was a turning point in the practical experiments with collective child rearing. Many who had worked in the Day Care Centers saw a dangerous tendency for the nonauthoritarian approach in preschool education to become an isolated activity in specific educational enclaves, attracting only a very limited portion of the population — particularly academics. For it became progressively clearer that the authoritarian capitalist methods of education could not be radically altered by bringing up a few middle class children in a nonauthoritarian way. One group in the Central Council, therefore, demanded that the socialist movement to mobilize workers focus on the work of left wing parents and educators and direct their efforts to the same end; for unless conducted in a worker-oriented framework, the attempts to create an alternative model of socialization within capitalism would only result in social enclaves.

After intensive discussions the Central Council — for a year the organizational and political focus of all the Day Care Centers — was dissolved. Some parent groups continued their activities with other left wing groups in West Berlin working class neighborhoods. A number of groups still exist which work in middle class communities, applying somewhat different ideas. This is not a final separation; some of the 20-odd groups which were still, in the spring of 1970, concerned with the education of their children, are now discussing whether to join a socialist organization.

Government Attempts to Integrate the New Education

The period is over when the principles of the Day Care Centers were viewed as nothing more than criminal subversion of state and family. The government's attempt to adopt the new child raising methods is analogous to the reform of higher education which was provoked by student revolts.

The first sign was a positive portrayal in the liberal press, notably the NDR (National German Radio) television broadcast, Gerhard Bott's "Educating Children to Disobedience," on December 1, 1969. After that, some Parent-Child Play Groups were formed through bourgeois initiative and received generous support from the Senate. Now many groups in universities, churches, and other institutions are trying to apply nonauthoritarian methods.

The history of the Day Care Centers and the fate of the new education demonstrates:

1. The potential for real change through the Day Care Center movement does not lie in confrontation with traditional preschool education as much as in political alliance with the left. The dynamics of its internal development also depend on political questions. The experiment stemmed not from our asking, "How can we better raise our children?" but from the questions, "How can we ourselves do more political work?" and "How can we do revolutionary work in education to mobilize people?"

2. Our late-capitalist society is too decayed to generate vital changes in education and culture. This applies to child care as much as to high schools, vocational schools, and universities; a revolutionary movement, at least a nominal one, is imperative to catalyze the necessary reforms.

State of Emergency in Preschool Education

By the end of the sixties the inadequacy of existing pre-school education, even in terms of the limited cultural and educational aims of formally democratic West Germany, was apparent to all serious observers. This was as true of education within the family as of that in public institutions.

These are no longer controversial statements:

> Since learning, not heredity, accounts for the bulk of human behavior, educational and environmental influences are crucial factors. Even bourgeois scholarship has finally conceded this. Now the liberal "progressive" mass media — for example, the magazine Der Stern — recognize that: "Juvenile delinquency is not an inexplicable phenomenon, it is a comprehensible fact. Children are not born criminal — they are made criminal. Parents, grandmothers, aunts, guidance counselors, judges, as well as the environment in which children grow up produce crime; in short, it depends on social conditions."
> — article on juvenile delinquency, Stern, 8.2.1970, p. 48

The basic patterns of social behavior are formed in the first stage of socialization. Again, we can quote Der Stern:

> Parents who tie their children to the potty, stick their noses in excrement, or beat them for soiling their pants, fail society in a serious way. They are raising their children to be helpless adults, model citizens who will obey orders opposed to their own needs — and do so meticulously. Despite the traditional German gospel, children are not naturally well behaved and polite; they are molded to display these qualities. And the cost of this achievement is the blocking of their instinctive drives . . . (ibid., p. 54).

The conflicts created by upbringing and environment lead, increasingly, to youthful apathy, crime, or neurosis.

In West Berlin and in the West German republic, the protest of kindergarten teachers originated in the intolerable conditions they found in public institutions. More and more, complaints concerned not only the absence of financial support, but the authoritarian methods. About 80 percent of teacher/student interchange consists of issuing orders and suggestions not open to contradiction — a fact not even apprehended by most teachers.
— *based on Tausch's research*

The crisis can no longer be concealed. The important question is why there has been no real change, although for years all responsible professionals and at least part of the general public have been well aware of the evil. Why are even the present reforms so fragmentary? Considering the potential of modern knowledge and technology, the blame must be assigned to a deeper level than the failure of individuals or parties.

Causes of the Poverty of Education

Despite the myth of a "developed society," a country of freedom and equal opportunity, a hierarchy of rich and poor, privileged and underprivileged, characterizes the German republic — with obvious implications for education. The increasing impoverishment of the majority and the increasing wealth of a minority is a demonstrable fact with far-reaching consequences. For example, the effect on the preschool education of different neighborhoods is evident in the data provided by the Senator in charge of Family, Youth, and Sport. In 1966 there were 29,897 children in both public and private kindergartens; and there was a waiting list of 19,600, which omits, of course, numerous parents who, in view of the shortage, did not bother to apply. In 1969 there were 32,500 children in government-owned kindergartens and 2,500 in others, totalling only one-quarter of all children between three and six and 8 percent of those under three. There will be no improvement in the foreseeable future. A Berlin Press Service article of May 29, 1969, runs:

There is also a shortage of places and personnel in Wedding. At present there are 1,956 places in the child care institutions of the district. 97 percent are needed for children of employed mothers and 3 percent are filled for pedagogical reasons. About 1,900 more applications are on file. Even the two new child

care centers will increase the number of available places for
1970 by only 232; and actually, the situation will deteriorate
with the opening of the new centers, for we will need 26 more
kindergarten teachers.

Conditions in Wedding and Kreuzberg are typical of working
class districts. A kindergarten teacher who complained to her
superiors about the intolerable conditions in Kreuzberg received
a cynical, and revealing, reply: "What do you expect?. Most of
these children will wind up in special schools anyway. Come
to Dahlem — in the better neighborhoods, you'll see that it's
entirely different."

Among the deciding factors in a child's growth are housing, the
mother's employment, public facilities, and so forth. These determine the destiny of the individual. Erich Wulff, surveying
6,000 out of 20,000 children, analyzed the conditions in which
the Kreuzberg working class grows up. In this district, every
eighth student does not possess a bed of his own. Every
third has nowhere to work at home and no corner in which to
play. Only one in ten has his own room. Almost 40 percent live in
houses without toilets or baths. Three-quarters live in one- to
two-room apartments; 39 percent live with a minimum of three
other persons, in apartments of one room and a kitchen. Thirty-
four percent of the mothers work and are out of the house up to
ten hours a day. Almost half of the children of working mothers
are "kids with keys," not cared for by neighbors, relatives, or
child care centers. Thus the material circumstances of work and
life, as well as the system of schooling, guarantee that workers
will be unable, in any significant numbers, to leave their class.

When workers' children begin school, they are already in-
tellectually underprivileged. These figures from a study by Cordt
are revealing; while children of academics, higher level officials,
and white collar workers prove through examinations to be
92 percent ready for school, 5 percent ready with some qualifications, and 3 percent not ready; the corresponding results for
children of skilled workers are 67 percent, 17 percent, and
16 percent; and for children of unskilled workers, 59 percent,
18 percent, and 23 percent. Moreover, the first category accounts
for under one-fifth of the total population (Padagogische Rundschau 1963, pp. 420 f.). Although the working class constitutes
half the general population, only 5 percent of university students

have a working class background. In addition, we must consider that, according to Bloom's frequently cited study, the development of intelligence is half accomplished by the age of four, and 80 percent completed by age eight.

Therefore, the cause of the present emergency in West German education is the class conflict which capitalism imposes on our society. This, as Marx pointed out, is the basic contradiction of capitalism: on the one hand, the economic system (mode of production) requires cooperation; the division of labor links the producers in an extended interdependence which makes possible the development of vast productive powers and collective wealth. On the other hand, the system is geared to private accumulation of property — while wealth is appropriated by the propertied class, the producers are virtually excluded from the reservoir of wealth and do not even perceive their own humanity in their "alienated" work. This basic contradiction is inherent in capitalism; it assumes specific forms at different historic stages. The central economic contradiction generates others in various areas of social organization, such as child care and education, housing, family life, financial planning, the military, etc.

Both the primary and the secondary contradictions are susceptible to objective investigation — they are not a matter of partisan scholarship or personal bias. The research done in our society, it is true, habitually tries to evade presenting the connection between the derivative problems and capitalism's fundamental contradiction, because research ultimately depends on ruling class interests. (For clarification, see E. Mandel, *Introduction to the Marxist Theory of Economics*, Frankfurt, 1967; and Mao Tse-Tung, "On Contradiction," *Selected Works*, vol. I, 1924-1937, China Books, San Francisco, 1970, pp. 311 f.)

In the German Federal Republic, education is a special area of crisis. The increase of productive capacity relies on complex technological improvement; and technological development requires heavy, long-term investment in education. Economic development demands of the individual producer more autonomy as well as increased flexibility in cooperation; it also requires a greater application of intelligence. But investment in education balks the short range profit drive, based on competition, characteristic of private capitalism. Thus the state serves as a buffer between capital and labor; it undertakes the job of padding the impact of the contradiction. Concretely, the state tries to improve the qualifications of labor by elaborating the economic infrastructure (cultural organizations, information, communications, channels of association). The state bears the collective costs necessary to make private profit. It acts to keep public misery (the correlative of private accumulation) from reaching the level at which it might threaten the smooth functioning of the capitalist system.

Anyone who takes educational problems seriously and does not merely wish — in the Social Democrats' manner — to tinker with the system, will conclude that the reform formula must be rejected, for it only reinforces the class structure by softening the harshest consequences of a secondary contradiction and obscuring the basic contradiction. Therefore, in the following chapters, we will consider and evaluate the aspects of the Day Care Center movement related to this fundamental contradiction.

In the long run, the fight against authoritarianism can succeed only by the elimination of existing controls over child raising and education. Only a proletariat-based organization can accomplish this, by means of a skillfully directed attack on all levels of the state apparatus. The struggle would have to begin with the fight of salaried workers on the economic marketplace.

Nowadays it is fashionable in academic circles to be radical. Many people realize that socialism is approaching a worldwide victory in our time, and they consider themselves Marxists because they wordily expound their critical insights on late-capitalist institutions. Their actions, however, go no further than, at best, opposing particular abuses in their own field of work. They repress the fact that political insight per se cannot produce change. What Mao Tse-Tung says of liberals applies to them:

> Liberalism originates in the selfish interests of the petty bourgeoisie: individual needs come first and those of the revolution second; the result is ideological, political and organizational liberalism. Liberals see fundamental Marxist propositions as abstract dogmas! They declare themselves supporters of Marxism, but they are unprepared to apply it — at least not in serious actions; they are not ready to replace liberalism with Marxism. These people have something of Marxism and something of liberalism: they have Marxism in their mouths, but liberalism in their minds; they face others as Marxists, but themselves as

liberals; they carry both kinds of wares, for each has its utility. Such is the thinking of some people.
— *Mao Tse-Tung, "Concerning Liberalism," Selected Works, vol. II, 1937-1941, p. 29*

The present book came out of the actions of the Day Care Center movement. It is the first in a series of studies of "collective child raising," and it presents the work of the West Berlin Day Care Centers from three perspectives: (1) their historical connection with the student movement; (2) the public reaction and its sociopolitical background; and (3) the program of nonauthoritarian child raising, the methods of working with groups of parents and of children, particularly in Charlottenburg I, a Day Care Center where the authors themselves were actively involved and which is still functioning in one of the West Berlin working class districts.

In order to illustrate the experience in process, the major documents for each chapter are printed separately; one can understand these documents in the historical context provided by our text.

Further studies on the theme of collective child raising will eventually include a systematic discussion of the theoretical foundations of nonauthoritarian child raising, a study of the historical precedents, and a careful inquiry into the growth of a children's collective.

West Berlin, 1970   *Katia Sedoun*

Valeria Schmidt

Eberhard Schultz

Storefront Day Care Centers

1. The Origin of the Day Care Centers Within the New Left

SDS and APO in February of 1968

The first Storefront Day Care Centers in West Berlin were founded on the initiative of the Women's Liberation Action Group. In February 1968, the women had begun discussing the problems involved in utilizing their time and energy in political work. What was happening then in the APO (extra-parliamentary opposition)? Why did women, especially those with children, feel they were excluded from political activity?

The murder of Benne Ohnesberg during a demonstration against the Shah of Iran on June 2, 1967, provoked massive student vigils and demonstrations — in planning and execution, these were cooperative efforts of SDS and various student organizations. Idealistic attempts to distribute pamphlets and to educate "the people" of Berlin about the demonstrations and their political background led to frustration and, after some months, to retreat, because the public did not respond in a political way. As a result of these experiences, the politically active initiated two projects: a campaign against Springer, the owner of a newspaper empire; and the creation of a nonofficial and critical "free university."

The Springer campaign was intended to mobilize the public against one of its chief manipulators and the most powerful enemy of the student movement.

The new free university was meant to enable students and young workers to organize actively and liberate themselves from the repressive conditions of academic life and to help them connect their studies with social reality.

Public political activity consisted primarily of teach-ins and demonstrations against the American war of aggression in Vietnam, clashes with the university bureaucracy, and occasional confrontations with the courts. SDS started several active study groups on higher education, labor, and the third world. All these groups did theoretical work in preparation for campaigns and political action. They used the literature (Marxist works, social criticism, factual material on special topics) to analyze existing conflicts and to plot strategy. The weekly SDS general meeting linked the groups; however, there was more planning for campaigns and actions than substantive discussion of committee studies.

The Berlin Vietnam demonstrations were significant. They usually ran the same course: first posters, pamphlets, and public notices called students from the universities and technical institutes to a mass demonstration on Saturday afternoon; then with red flags, bullhorns, speeches, and chants, the demonstrators took the usual route through the city; and after the demonstration was officially over, most of the marchers hurried to the Kurfurstendamm (the Fifth Avenue or Champs Elysées of Berlin) for the second act. Part of the group gathered at the Kranzler corner to distribute pamphlets and talk to people; the rest waited for the weekly epilogue — the confrontation with the police, who were equipped with clubs and hoses to disperse the talkers and maintain "peace and order."

Comment: The Meaning of the "Brawls"

Even at the time, these ritual demonstrations were sharply criticized within the movement. Some observers said they lacked political perspective and that, although the protesters claimed an abstract identification with the Viet Cong, in reality they were only fighting the police. On the other hand, the police and the popular press overestimated the demonstrations, terming them revolts, riots, and uprisings. Yet at least the popular press understood that there was more to these traffic disruptions than a brawl with the police, an event unlikely to be useful to anyone.

The popular press said that Vietnam was only an excuse for the students, an excuse for disturbing the peace. Moral objections to American Vietnam policy were but a mask for the real goal — an attack on the internal security of Berlin, a disruption of public order, and an attempt to overthrow the very structure of society. Thus the hostile press, while intending to denounce the movement, actually clarified the political connections which were disappearing in the protesters' oratory. From the press the students could learn that it was not enough just to stimulate the public to concern about Vietnam; that they were actually fighting the state machinery; that their assertions of solidarity with the third world liberation movement could have meaning only insofar as they attacked the law and order imposed by the ruling class bureaucracy. The papers also allowed them to discover that paralyzing the Kurfurstendamm was not exactly, despite Springer's suggestions, the ultimate limit of war on the state.

— *Decline of the Popular Press*,
SDS/KU Writers' Collective, 1969, pp. 122 f.

In this period, there was another phenomenon which neither right nor left wing critics could account for: the fact that the weekly brawls on the Kurfurstendamm consistently attracted new groups and individuals to politics.

The slogan of Commune 1, that revolution must be fun, offended right and left wing alike; the former considered lack of seriousness sacrilegious, and the latter thought no amount of fun could replace political judgment. It seemed as if the students were swallowing the propaganda of the sensationalist papers; they were being goaded to repeat their actions and were thus giving all their attention to a trivial target. The abstract contrast between repetition compulsion and political wisdom, however, explained little — certainly not why this weekly ritual accomplished at least as much as political education in widening the movement's student base.

But when viewed as a form of psychoanalytic repetition, a dialectical concept, these brawls on the Kurfurstendamm appear in another light: in this sense, repetition may be the decisive tool in clearing away inner resistance, a process beyond the scope of an individual's memory or a political group's reasoning. In this perspective, we can see why the much criticized demonstration game was still popular and continually mobilized new groups. Conflicts from family and school, long forgotten and repressed experiences of physical threats, were recreated under new conditions. This sort of experience was altered in the repetition, for the individual's confrontation with force, formerly resolvable only by identification with the oppressor, could now be relived as a collective experience. Even the frustration inevitable in such games with an overwhelming counter-force was undergone collectively and thus differed from that so familiar to each as an individual. Police authority was of another type than that which one had long ago, for the sake of survival, internalized. In collective resistance to police violence, insult, scorn, and ridicule burst out of the realm of fantasy and were actually vented on the authority. In attacking the police, and even in running away, one experienced not only fear and guilt, but also a heightened state of physical and mental functioning, more formidable weapons against one's own internalized enemies than against the forces of the state. In the anonymity of the crowd the subjective energy of the individual was not crushed, as bourgeois thinkers resentfully claim; rather, it was freed. Considering that spontaneous action, collective initiative, and mass action based on self-organization became real possibilities rather than topics for discussion, we can see how vast was the energy released in the crowd through the liberation of individuals from inner repression.

— SDS/KU Writers' Collective, *op. cit.*, pp. 120 f.

The Commune as Counter-Family

Commune 1 tried, by coming together to demonstrations, to offer a model of liberated conduct. Above all, communality was to be extended to "private life." The program of Commune 1, and the fascination it held for others, was the promise of a new kind of communal life capable of ending individual repression. Close communal living in political groups was meant to end the separation of political and private life, a result of capitalistic exploitation and division of labor, and the separation of work and residence places. This separation, familiar in the huge universities, had constantly troubled the students in their earlier political actions: the solidarity found while planning and carrying out demonstrations tended to die out in the isolated life of student housing. In 1967, two groups, later named Communes 1 and 2, actually attempted to combine communal life with collective work.

The communes gained their initial public reputation at the university and in Berlin through their guerilla theater. Commune 1 became notorious for their concept of fun, their provocatively insulting pamphlets, and for the model of noncoercive group unity they presented in public actions. In May 1967, Commune 1 was expelled from SDS because of a provocative "ruffling maneuver," incompatible with SDS tactics, during an organizational meeting at the university. After this episode the political organization suppressed public discussion of the communes. Consequently, some members knew nothing at first about the important job Commune 1 did in the fight against the judicial system as they ridiculed the antiquated machinery of repression simply by rejecting the role of cowed defendant (as described in Commune 1's pamphlets, especially "Steal Me").

Commune 2, founded as an SDS collective in February 1967, also withdrew that summer from active participation in SDS politics. This group was studying theoretical and practical psychoanalysis, along the guidelines of Wilhelm Reich, in order to work out a method of taking the individual's work and love problems, shaped by the bourgeois family, and resolving them through the group. This would make possible effective work in a political collective. They were involved, in theory and practice, in nonrepressive ways of bringing up the commune's children.

At the beginning of 1968, therefore, the political activities of the Berlin SDS membership (campaign for the National Liberation Front; conflicts in the university; labor relations; campaigns against the judicial system and against Springer) were not yet visibly connected with the "private" problems of communal life, including the role of women and child raising.

Day Care Centers Begin at the Vietnam Congress
February 1968

"We are in danger of seeing ourselves only as a remote branch of the Liberation Front and our actions only as symbolic attacks on imperialism, instead of concretely fighting imperialism . . . . What matters is whether we fight the oppressors in our own country . . . ."

With these words, radical students and youth were called from all over Western Europe and the United States to the Vietnam Congress in West Berlin, February 18 to 21, 1968; there were thousands in the large auditorium of the Technical University. There were speeches filled with revolutionary fervor, frequent bursts of enthusiastic applause, and extended chants. Refusal of permission for a planned demonstration, and the fascist reaction of the Springer press, intensified feelings of unity between German and foreign groups. For once, we didn't feel like a "small radical minority."

In the lobby of the Technical University, on the periphery of the major event, about 40 participants' children were playing.

The women of the Action Group had gotten tired of looking on from the sidelines. During the Congress and the demonstration they organized a kindergarten staffed by parents and volunteers, so that all those who usually would have had to stay home to babysit could participate in the Congress. The children, instead of being pushed around in the crowd, frightened and isolated, were suddenly free to share with the adults the excitement of the hour. They made flags from rags and played "demonstration." Parents, especially mothers, discovered for the first time that their family problem was not necessarily a private one. The Women's Liberation Action Group showed the way to a collective solution. Similarly marginal to the major event was Commune 2's publication of a pamphlet about a "model of nonauthoritarian education" based on the principles of Vera Schmidt's Moscow Child Care Laboratory. The introduction said:

We can start with Vera Schmidt's experiment in the Moscow Child Care Laboratory and develop our own ideas of collective nonrepressive child rearing, ideas which can be taught to the masses. . . .

Let's avoid one misunderstanding: a counter-institution such as a Day Care Center based on psychoanalytic theory cannot simply change society by example. That requires a long-term political fight, the overthrow of repressive institutions, and the transfer of the means of production into the hands of the entire society. But in this fight counter-institutions can play an important role by calling into question that one-dimensional consciousness which sees existing conditions as absolutely unchangeable. Counter-institutions can also allow "Sunday Socialists" to use their educational background to make a real contribution.

We think that republishing Vera Schmidt's report, which is related to our own experiments in collective living, is the first step toward a practical goal: the initiation of similar experiments in West Berlin and the Federal Republic.

— (cf. this volume, Documents, pp. 16 ff.)

Theory in the Student Movement

In the following pages we will sketch the political theories underlying the various areas of activity within the student movement; in other words, the revolutionary framework that linked its diverse aspects. From our present viewpoint, we cannot do this without first stating some ideas and experiences which have since become the common property of all socialist groups.

The seemingly diverse areas of revolutionary work all stemmed from the same source: the existential experience of oppression and alienation in work (especially in higher education) and in private life. Although previously this had led inexorably to individual withdrawal, such as truancy or dropping out, the situation changed at the end of the period of German economic reconstruction with the subsequent intensification of social contrasts. The economic recession of 1966–1967 and public oppression by ideological manipulation and realignment led to the reactionary politics of the SPD (German Socialist Party), with its coalition politics and "Emergency Measures." These developments and the study of third world liberation movements made us aware of the societal processes behind our own individual unhappiness. Radical groups came to believe that active intervention in societal processes would also result in an improvement of personal situations.

But why, then, did students and marginal youth groups begin their revolt when they seemed to lack the support of the general population? The New Left answered with a new theory of revolution:

> *If Marx saw in the proletariat the revolutionary class, he did so also, and maybe even primarily, because the proletariat was free from the repressive needs of capitalist society, because the new needs for freedom could develop in the proletariat and were not suffocated by the old, dominant ones. Today in large parts of the most highly developed capitalist countries that is no longer the case. The working class no longer represents the negation of existing needs.*
> — Herbert Marcuse, "The End of Utopia," in *Five Lectures*, Boston: Beacon Press, 1970, p. 70

From this analysis follows the conclusion that today's working class is not ready to fight. Marcuse then moves to his theory of marginal groups, which assigns the intelligentsia, especially students, a new function in the revolutionary movement.

The role of students today as the intelligentsia out of which, as you know, the executives and leaders even of existing society are recruited, is historically more important than it perhaps was in the past. In addition there is the moral-sexual rebellion, which turns against the dominant morality and must be taken seriously as a disintegrative factor, as can be seen from the reaction to it, especially in the United States. Finally, probably, here in Europe we should add those parts of the working class that have not yet fallen prey to the process of integration. Those are the tendential forces of transformation, . . . (ibid., p. 71).

It is easy enough today to spot the idealistic, erroneous assumptions behind the theory of marginal groups. Nevertheless, in its time, the "reappraisal of subjective factors" had a significant effect in the courage it gave to isolated groups to attack an apparently unshakeable social structure, consolidated during the years of economic reconstruction and Cold War propaganda. Now this revolutionary theory gave substance to the challenge: The time is ripe for revolution! We no longer have to wait for the third world movement to have an impact on the advanced countries. In practical terms, the students could turn to Professor Marcuse's paternal justification of anarchist rebellion:

But I believe that there is a "natural right" of resistance for oppressed and overpowered minorities to use extralegal means if the legal ones have proved to be inadequate. Law and order are always and everywhere the law and order which protect the established hierarchy; it is nonsensical to invoke the absolute authority of this law and this order against those who suffer from it and struggle against it — not for personal advantages and revenge, but for their share of humanity. There is no other judge over them than the constituted authorities, the police, and their own conscience. If they use violence, they do not start a new chain of violence but try to break an established one.

— (Marcuse, in *A Critique of Pure Tolerance*,
Boston: Beacon Press, 1965, pp. 116-117

Since the marginal group theory claims to be the creative continuation of Marxist social thought and since it is still used, in various guises, as theoretical support for the Day Care Center movement and other practical political projects, especially those dealing with children in institutions, reform schoolers, and victims of the courts, it seems important to expose the erroneous assumption upon which the theory depends. But first we must examine the theory more closely. Marcuse, unintentionally, provides a clue in his discussion of the development of contradictions in society:

Today the classical contradictions within capitalism are stronger than they have ever been before. Especially the general contradiction between the unprecedented development of the productive forces and social wealth on the one hand and of the destructive and repressive application of these forces of production on the other is infinitely more acute today than it has ever been.
— Marcuse, "The End of Utopia," in *Five Lectures*, p. 70

In the process of defining this "classic contradiction," Marcuse makes a significant distortion: he turns the basic contradiction in capitalism between cooperative production of wealth and private appropriation of it, between wage labor and capital, into a contradiction between forces of production and destructive state machinery. No longer do two classes embody the decisive contrast; rather, there is a single oppressed humanity which can and must fight the destructive bureaucratic machinery.

The marginal group theory was elucidated for German students by Rudi Dutschke, who applied it, in *Rebellion of the Students*, to the revolt in higher education. He began with the idea that "the industrial bureaucracy" is a "new class" which "accomplishes the repressive desocialization of capital":

This is both the strongest and the weakest feature of the advanced stage of capitalism. No group remains outside the framework of repression; all are to be ruled by a "system of concepts within the capitalist framework" (Sering). The structure is supported by the "silent force of circumstances" and by the internalized norms and ideas of bourgeois-capitalist society. But when an underprivileged faction essential to the proper functioning of the system bursts out of the "complicity of interest groups" to which the social product is politically "distributed," out of the "tacitly accepted limitation of interests and needs in accordance with the ruling framework," then the entire system is challenged.
— Rudi Dutschke, *Rebellion of the Students*, Hamburg, 1968, p. 89

The left wing movement in West Berlin and the Federal Republic reached some practical conclusions:

> Our historically justified focus on university life must not become a fetish. A revolutionary dialectic must comprehend the need for practical and theoretical action by choosing the right series of steps on the "long march through the institutions"; the goal is to heighten, by subversive criticism, the existing contradictions in all institutions involved in the organization of daily life. In this phase of the cultural revolution, there is no longer a single group exclusively suited to voice the interests of the entire movement.
>
> — Rudi Dutschke, op. cit., p. 89

The students' voluntaristic approach characterizes this cultural revolution: "The outcome of this historical period depends primarily on our will."

Critique of the Revolutionary Theory of This Period

Within the left wing of that time, one can distinguish two separate interpretations of the student movement: the theory of marginal groups and the theory of the intelligentsia as a productive force. However, in justifying action, the two were freely mixed.

1. *The theory of marginal groups* depends, as we have indicated in our brief sketch, on the theory of the authoritarian state. According to the latter theory, class conflict is diminishing, and precisely because of that phenomenon, students can be a decisive element in the transformation of society. Because they stand outside the capitalistic production process, they constitute, it was often said, the most conscious part of the population, the part best able to perceive the interconnectedness of the forces of oppression.

2. *The theory of the intelligentsia as a productive force*, on the other hand, declared that the requirements of production at an advanced stage of capitalism govern, ever more directly, the options in study and research. Therefore, the situation of the students increasingly approaches that of the proletariat.

Since both interpretations see students as an indivisible entity, politicizing them becomes purely an educational matter: they only need instruction to make them cognizant of either their own interests as exploited producers or of the real interests of human beings up against the authoritarian state. Neither interpretation offers a workable definition of the student/worker relationship.

Critique of the Marginal Group Theory

The basic premise of this theory, that research functions to meet the requirements of monopoly capitalism, implies a correlate, that research can be a ruling element in society. Holding technological power, the student or scholar stands on the fringe of the manipulated masses, outside the production process involving his research. Therefore, he is a potential revolutionary. The facts appeared to bear out this assumption: students and others marginal to the economy, but not workers, rose up to challenge the society. This thesis concerning the power of technology amounts to saying that the primary contradiction between labor and capital has been transformed into a contradiction between the state machinery and the individual. Revolutionaries fall into the "absurd position of fighting the actual machinery, rather than the ways in which capitalism applies it" (Marx, *Capital* I, *Works* 4, Darmstadt, 1962, p. 515). This was the theoretical support for the student movement's strategy in all actions outside the university. In *Analysis of the Student Movement*, Schmierer examines the effects of this theory on practical politics:

The marginal group theory, beginning with the contradiction between impersonal machinery and oppressed humanity, inevitably arrived at the strategy of a wave of general enlightenment, starting with marginal groups but eventually engulfing all human beings, all those previously inhibited from rising up against the state machinery only by a false perception of reality. Thus, the organization now crushing humanity would topple like a house of cards. It was on this premise that Rudi Dutschke proclaimed the "long march through the institutions" and called for a united attack on all forms of authority, while asserting that, in advanced countries, armed confrontation was an obsolete tactic.
— Schmierer, Red Press Communication, #42, p. 13

Critique of the Theory of Research as a Productive Force

The theory of research as a productive force, from which derives the concept of a new working class, was created to explain and justify the student movement. The student revolt, in this theory, would shortly become an attack on the very institutions in which the students would later hold jobs. In reality, however,

*all attempts to organize the members of the superstructure pro-
fessions (teaching, law) in a socialist movement came to nothing.
One can explain the student movement in terms of the height-
ening of social contrasts at the end of the period of German economic reconstruction . . . but not by invoking the significance
of research and study as productive forces. So far the student
movement has found a mass base only in the humanities departments and has had little success in the natural sciences and technical fields. As is obvious to many students, the material taught
in the humanities is patent nonsense; but there used to be a
mitigating factor — the chance for individual escape, either
through involvement in poetry and art, or through the apparent
freedom of choice in research. But the possible avenues of escape
diminished with the trend to formalize higher education (limiting
length of study, screening university study by mass exams and
formal projects, clever manipulation of power by the university
administration). Curriculum reform and legislation dealing with
higher education finally eliminated all escape options. The student
movement, up to that point, had not been the revolt of a productive
force engaged in research, but the protest of a conceited "free
intelligentsia" which came to the jarring realization that organized
society would not detour reverently around it, that protests against
the war in Vietnam and the Emergency Legislation, as well as
disgust with the bourgeois life style, would no longer be tolerated,
for the forces that shape society require that universities produce
a supply of ideological spokesmen.*
    — Schmierer, Red Press Communication, #42, p. 11

 The theory that the research segment was revolting as an
exploited productive force could, and did, however, provide an
identity for the rebel students. Only when the students attempted
to extend the strategies of university revolt and to become
professional revolutionaries did they discover the difficulties
of the theory, the obstacles to their attempts to politicize petit
bourgeois intellectuals. In the meantime, the more general theories
surrounding the idea of research as a productive force had
distorted rather than illuminated the students' problems.
 Both these simplistic explanations of the left wing movement
arose from the students' need to see their own revolt as the seed
of total revolution. Hence the need to interpret the students'
situation within the capitalist structure as a representative one;
both theories met this need. But only the marginal group theory

could lead "in materialist terms" to a revolutionary strategy. The false generalizations in both theories made them dangerous when the forms and conditions of confrontation had visibly altered: the official counter-attempt to integrate the masses in education (reform of technocratic higher education) increased the pressure on the political students, while concurrently, with the intensification of the class struggle in Western Europe, it became both possible and necessary to define the student/worker relationship.

The revolt of the students, in fact, can only be explained in terms of the university situation and capitalism's devaluation of scholarship. In summary, we can say this: in certain historical situations marginal groups can initiate the revolutionary transformation of society, and in the last few years, the students have been doing exactly this; but it is an error of theory to suppose that marginal groups can carry a revolution any further. Because the student group is not, objectively, an oppressed faction, it was forced to borrow class consciousness from the workers. Only the workers, however, are objectively (1) forced to sell their only asset — their capacity for labor; (2) dependent on, and directly oppressed by, the production requirements of monopoly capitalism; and (3) the producers of profit (surplus value). These points outline the working class situation and constitute necessary, though not sufficient, preconditions of working class consciousness.

The student does not have to sell his labor; he is fighting only the tendency of the commodity structure of society to dictate the circumstances of his life and study. Students are fighting the force which turns *them* into commodities, but not, fundamentally, the commodity orientation of society. Hence, despite its occasional aggressive tactics, the essentially defensive, ad hoc character of the student movement. This borrowed class consciousness explains the movement's failure to fulfill the two basic needs of a revolutionary movement: spontaneous mass action and revolutionary organization.

The students lack an objective, shared class interest. Their spontaneous actions, for this reason, tend to end in individual flight or the liberation of small groups.

An enormous leap in the number of drop-outs preceded the student movement, and the movement was partly a matter of mobilizing and uniting these drop-outs; it is hard for the

movement to transcend its initial character. This is evident even
now in the common feeling that the individual, as such, can
evade capitalistic pressures by withdrawing, an attitude which
definitely impedes organization.

— Red Press Communication, #48, p. 9

Effect of the Theory and Practice of the
Student Movement on the Day Care Centers

The Day Care Centers began in that phase of the movement
when political action was shifting from the universities to life
outside them. Since the marginal group theory did not stimulate
a comprehensive revolutionary strategy, any group that wished
to attack, through criticism, any part of the system, could consider itself part of the nebulous APO (extra-parliamentary
opposition). The movement's thinking at that time was best
characterized by Rudi Dutschke: "In this phase of the cultural
revolution, there is no longer a single group exclusively suited
to voice the interests of the entire movement." At the same time,
each particular group considered its own work the decisive form
of revolutionary activity. This paradox affected the development
of the Day Care Centers, which, from the beginning, thought of
themselves as part of the APO.

Documents A

Introduction to
PSYCHOANALYTIC EDUCATION IN THE SOVIET UNION:
REPORT OF THE MOSCOW CHILD CARE LABORATORY
by Vera Schmidt

In general, the rebellion of students and youth against authoritarianism derives from a psychic tension which our social situation only aggravates. Given the total wealth of our society, rigorous repression of the instincts seems absurd, yet it is forced on people by a system of production and distribution that is geared not to meet the needs of the population, but to reinforce class differences and class rule. The absolute respect for private property, coupled with the fact of material superabundance, makes stealing about the only rational form of acquisition. The transition to a communist society, in which each is given what he needs, has long been economically possible. Yet society still expects the individual to acquire possessions only in reward for survival in competition within the economic hierarchy. The adjustment to instinctual renunciation, to holding boring, meaningless, and petty jobs in giant bureaucracies, subjects the individual to an ever more intolerable strain.

The family still makes the first conquest over infantile instincts. But the early conflicts between social reality and physiological pleasure can no longer be adequately expressed by rebellion against parents alone. The actual weakness of the father in society, due to the decline of free competition and individual enterprise, makes it almost impossible to confront personally the restrictive authority that demands suppression of instincts. Because of the father's visible helplessness against the forces that govern the entire society, son can no longer identify with father. "From his relationship with his father, the child learns only an abstract concept of arbitrary force and he seeks a mightier father than his real one. . . . The father is replaced by powerful groups — the class of peers in school, the world of sport, the social gathering, and, finally, the state" (*Sociological Excursus*, p. 127).

In other words, institutions other than the family (mass media, advertising, school) assume an increasing share of the task of adapting the child to social norms. Two significant consequences are: (1) Formerly, when the clash between instincts and social norms was enacted by individuals within the bourgeois family, the result might be, in exceptional cases, an individual of considerable ego strength and autonomy. But there can be no such individual confrontation with the remote models of behavior that appear in movies, television, and advertising. The only way a child can assume the strength of these models is self-surrender through identification. The ego, which requires conflict in order to grow, stays dependent and weak. (2) Since the techniques used to make the masses adjust are uniform and impersonally imposed, they cannot be adapted to individual biological differences. Because individuals no longer transmit roles, it is now impossible subtly to bring people into line with those roles.

Aimless Aggression

The weakness of the individual ego makes intensified psychological pressure close to intolerable. But the aggression thus accumulated has no object. Since the individual has not developed, in personal confrontation, a specific negative image of the frustrating authority, he can only experience an abstract and generalized rebellion. Only too readily the rebel can find in himself a longing simply to give in to seemingly omnipotent social forces. This tendency explains why politically conscious groups have trouble progressing from mere rebellion against repression to the creation of a real political movement.

The Family's Resistance to Change

The sociological clichés about the family's shrinking role often obscure the fact of the family's remarkable ability to hang on stubbornly to its function as chief educator. The trend toward systematizing human relationships in order to manage and manipulate people has not yet been able to encompass early childhood, to include the idea of indoctrinating children from the first year. The insistence that the family must be the basic unit of society is, in fact, caused by the insoluble contradictions of capitalism. Thus:

1. A private profit economy does not give the state enough surplus money to finance collective education of small children in special institutions. The family, from the point of view of private enterprise, is still society's cheapest educational institution.

2. Only the family can perform the specific kind of repression which sets, in early childhood, the irrational roots for a deeply competitive attitude; thus it prepares the psychic ground for individual estrangement. This early, barriers are raised to prevent solidarity and unified revolt by the oppressed.

First, there is the competition between children and adults; second, the more intense competition between siblings for the attention and favor of parents. In childhood, this competition, later to be transformed into adult economic competition, is expressed mainly through highly charged hate-love relationships within the family.
— W. Reich, The Mass Psychology of Fascism, *p. 86*

3. As Reich has stressed, the triangular structure of the nuclear family, whether the parents be strict or permissive, in itself imposes a degree of authoritarianism on the child's personality. The small child, obliged to direct his sexual and affective energies solely towards his parents, "is oppressed by parental authority if only by virtue of his physical smallness" (Reich, *The Sexual Revolution*, III). The affective drives (in the Oedipal situation, love of the parent of the other sex and hate of the parent of the same sex) cannot be really worked through. Without a children's collective, in which the child can direct his sexual energies toward other children, these drives must be repressed almost completely. Unconscious guilt and anxiety intensify his fixation on his parents, which creates dependency, longing for powerful leaders, submission to authority and, in general, an "authoritarian personality."

4. If society took the responsibility for child rearing, social energies (especially women's) which are still bound up in child rearing would be freed. But considering the dearth of satisfying, meaningful jobs, these energies could easily seek a form of expression which would jeopardize the existing society.

5. Individuals in the face of the threatening forces of a vast society seek asylum in the family as a last pocket of human concern and warmth. Compared with existing state facilities for preschool children, which are not designed for collective education but as a stopgap replacement for scarce family resources, the traditional family may well seem preferable.

Need for Models

The irrationality of choosing the family as the nucleus of child raising reflects the irrationality of an entire society, which, despite its power to abolish suffering and oppression almost completely, tends to perpetuate physical suffering through war and to produce psychic disturbance through the ever more massive pressures of urban life. The irrational fears inculcated in early childhood produce the authoritarian character who longs above all for "security" and who tenaciously resists every radical movement for social change.

The nonrepressive movement must learn to take into account the longing for security; it must know how to work effectively with the fears of the masses at the psychological level, how to uncover their unconscious sources in the early experiences of repression and how to turn irrational aggression into the impetus for a rational transformation of society. Hence it is crucial to try to work out actual models of nonrepressive communal life.

Utopia as a Possibility

If society is not always to deny the proletariat, to reject the negative image of its material well-being as a testament to "a misery aware that it is misery" (Marx and Engels, *The Holy Family*), the transformation will demand a higher state of individual political consciousness than has ever been known.

Our capitalist society is already decadent; even now its revolutionary potential is decaying (Trotsky); and it is marked, above all, by the disparity between potentiality and actuality. Voluntaristic political groups must use this discrepancy for change. They must counter the seemingly immutable reality with alternatives proved to be possible and practical. Throughout history, inexorable social realities have always overshadowed utopias; but today, prototypes of future forms of organization can be productive factors in shaping a new society. Kautsky's aphorism, "We have no business concocting recipes for the future from the raw ingredients we find now," makes less sense now than ever before.

The psychological fears caused in childhood which block any hope of escape from a one-dimensional existence can be rechanneled and dedicated to a movement that can establish operating social models such as communes, free universities, and schools, which more adequately satisfy emotional and sexual desires. A large-scale attempt to deliberately transform aggression and fear, by tracing them to their source in infancy, might free the psychic energies needed to change this society.

The idea of collective, nonrepressive education, starting with Vera Schmidt's work, can be meaningfully communicated to large numbers of people. Stalin's version of industrialization stamped out her experiment, along with other models of a freer communal life. But for us, living in an era in which technological capacity could reduce work time to a bare minimum, it is not as a utopian dream, but as a real possibility, that we envisage a form of education which no longer strives mainly to internalize the drive to achieve, but to satisfy instinctual needs in a completely nonrepressive way.

Let's avoid one misunderstanding: a counter-institution such as a Day Care Center based on psychoanalytic theory cannot simply change society by example. That requires a long-term political fight, the overthrow of repressive institutions, and the transfer of the means of production into the hands of the entire society. But counter-institutions can play an important role in this fight by calling into question that one-dimensional consciousness which sees existing conditions as absolutely unchangeable. Counter-institutions can also allow "Sunday Socialists" to use their educational background to make a real contribution.

They can set an example and be a source of energy for subversive groups who can find in them inspiration and refuge. But such models must be part of a political movement in order to constitute a challenge to existing institutions and to use the antagonistic reaction of the establishment to develop the political consciousness of the people.

*   *   *

We think that republishing Vera Schmidt's report, which is related to our own experiments in collective living, is the first step toward a practical goal: to spread such models through West Berlin and all Germany. Perhaps then events might verify Wilhelm Reich's opinion of the Moscow Child Care Laboratory: "Still, in the history of education, Vera Schmidt was the first to try to apply the theory of infantile sexuality. Although on a smaller scale, her attempt is comparable in historical significance to the Paris Commune."

Berlin, February 1968

FOUNDING PROGRAM OF THE SCHONEBERG CENTER

1. Fundamental Propositions

The goal of all education performed in the family, preschool, school, and university, is to produce blind submission to the status quo.

The present hierarchical arrangement of education (from elementary to higher education) does not foster the full realization of individual potential in a society fit for human beings; it functions to perpetuate the existing order. Labor is trained for the jobs that exist and the ruling class decides what those should be. That class must necessarily concern itself with securing its position; it does so by manipulation. The power of rulers over subjects is camouflaged so that the ruled should not realize that society is interested in getting the greatest possible profit for those in power, not in providing for the needs of the people. (Hence the deliberate loss of capital through wars, superfluous products, and planned obsolescence.)

Nursery schools as we know them are like cemeteries: they bury the child's natural character and instill a hypocritical gentility and an archaic sense of decorum. The tenor of all education is adjustment to and acclamation of the status quo. As early as possible, the questioning of existing conditions must be silenced. As the twig is bent....

What facilitates repression in existing preschool institutions?

Note: Footnotes for this section appear on page 22.

Rigid forms of education: (a) false, rigid and outmoded teaching; relatively underpaid, poorly trained personnel; too many children per teacher;[1] (b) cramped and usually unsuitable facilities;[2] and (c) the demand that the child adjust to ever larger groups, which makes social and considerate behavior harder for him. That produces aggression, which is then suppressed by coercion. Because of overcrowding, the child cannot get the personal attention he needs. These conditions necessarily perpetuate repression.[3]

In self-defense, the teacher resorts to force and coercion (whether direct or subtle); but beyond this, he himself has been conditioned by upbringing and professional training to believe that order is the main responsibility of every citizen! Question: who profits from this vicious circle?

Constant supervision and endless commands and requests stifle creativity, stunt the unfolding of intelligence and initiative, and keep the child dependent.[4] *Nagging:* "Eat with your spoon ... No, use the other hand ... Don't slurp ... Shake hands with the nice lady ... No, the right hand ... What do you say? ... Hello and goodbye ... What do you say when you get a present? ... Don't get dirty ... Don't play with your food ... Don't ask so many questions ... Don't be so noisy ..." etc. *Persecution:* "Lazybones! ... Go stand in the corner! ... Johnny wet his bed! ... Ooh, ooh, aren't you ashamed? Everybody is staring at you ... I'm going to tell your Mommy about this ... Go stand outside" ... etc.

And so the system is perpetuated by hurting anyone who refuses to cooperate, who is "different," who represents a minority. This is how people are trained to compete and achieve. One must repress the child to produce a submissive adult; this is the rule that makes the machine run.

Conclusions
We will not play the game.

Founding nonrepressive kindergartens is practical action upon our political beliefs.

Our philosophy of human upbringing can have lasting meaning only if we develop models integrated into the total social process.

Therefore, we must attach our work and study groups to the Student Federation of Social Democrats (SDS). SDS is the political center of the nonrepressive movement and the founder of these kindergartens. Founding our own day care centers is only the beginning of a counter-culture; we must then start free schools and antiestablishment universities. We can create feasible forms of education for ourselves and our children and so demonstrate that the utopia of a society constructed for human beings is possible.

Proposals
The kindergartens should work on a minimum of bureaucracy; problems should be solved by common sense and direct human communication. We

don't want another establishment. Since our goals for our children require specific environmental conditions which are unprecedented, we must work out our own plan. We can only partially accept the concepts of A. S. Neill[5] and Vera Schmidt.[6]

We can use the relevant progressive literature to work out theoretical plans before we actually begin working. These plans must then be tested experimentally. We are essentially concerned with three domains: eating, sleeping, and playing. We must raise some radical questions about bourgeois eating and sleeping rituals. Our model should give the children optimum satisfaction of both desires and physiological needs. We must stop submitting to the consumer culture.

Since the present society cannot satisfy our fundamental needs, consumerism is only a substitute gratification. Our refusal to be manipulated consumers must carry over to designing and equipping the centers. We must also question the ideal of transferring our aesthetic standards to the children. The solution is improvisation and imperfection — using materials that originally had other functions for our furniture and toys (orange crates, boxes, tires, wood scraps for blocks, etc.). These materials are so cheap that we need not be concerned about damaging or breaking them and we can also make frequent changes. We can be sure that the environment will change with the children's needs.

Notes

1. *Die Zeit*, no. 50, 1968. Valeska von Roque's article on studies conducted by Anne-Marie Taush. Her tapes and films, made in urban kindergartens, demonstrated incontrovertibly the extreme authoritarian behavior of the teachers.
2. Report of the West Berlin Senate (1968!). In the plans for new Day Care Centers, 33 children are allotted 65 sq. yds. of space (2 sq. yds. per child; in Sweden the rule is at least 10 sq. yds. per child!).
3. Cf. René A. Spitz and W. G. Cobliner, *The First Year of Life*, International Universities Press, New York, 1966.
4. Cf. Lawrence S. Kubie, *Neurotic Distortion of the Creative Process*, Farrar, Strauss, and Giroux, New York, 1961, Chapter III.
5. Cf. A. S. Neill, *Summerhill: A Radical Approach to Child Rearing*, Hart Publishing Company, New York, 1970.
6. Vera Schmidt, *Education Without Repression*, on nonauthoritarian education (pamphlet put out by SDS, Berlin, 1968).

RESOLUTION OF THE ACTION COUNCIL, READ AT
SDS CONFERENCE IN FRANKFURT, SUMMER 1968

Comrades:

I represent the Action Council of Women's Liberation. The Berlin chapter of SDS gave me the chance to be a delegate, although only a few of us belong to SDS. We are here today because we know our work can only be accomplished by cooperating with progressive organizations, and right now, we think that only SDS counts.

But there can be no cooperation until SDS recognizes and understands the specific problems of women, which means that conflicts which SDS has long suppressed must be brought into the open. Therefore, we would encourage a confrontation between the antirepressive and the Communist Party factions of SDS and we would oppose both, since in action, though not in words, both oppose us. We shall try to state our position clearly. We demand a substantive discussion of our problems. We are no longer content to have "liberated" men allow us to say a few words occasionally and then pass, unconcerned, to the agenda for the day.

We have observed that the internal relationships of SDS are the mirror image of the workings of society at large. Everyone, however, tries not to see the gap between claim and reality, for facing up to this would mean revising SDS policy. It is easy to avoid mention of this discrepancy by excluding that area from social life, labelling it taboo and private. The taboo that SDS uses is indistinguishable from the one at work in labor unions and political parties. The exploitative relationships in which women are trapped are never mentioned, so that the men need not renounce the identity they defined in the patriarchal days. Certainly, women are allowed to speak; but no one asks why they do so little, why they are so passive, why they follow policies set by the organization but seldom help to create them. (On the first day of this conference, one woman spoke.)

The facts can be suppressed gracefully by pointing to the exceptional woman, active in the organization, who has achieved some status. No one wonders what renunciations she had to make; no one considers the fact that she had to adjust to a competitive principle of striving for individual achievement which is exactly what men are trying to abolish because it is destroying them. That kind of emancipation is merely equal submission to injustice, an equality to be achieved by the precise means we reject — competition and the principle of individual achievement.

The separation between private and public life always forces the woman into lonely endurance of the problems of her role. She is still being raised to play wife and mother, in a family which is patterned to fit the economic structure of society which we most want to change. The role she is taught, the sense of inferiority which is cultivated in her, the disparity between her hopes and society's demands generate a perpetual feeling of guilt. She always feels incapable of doing what is asked of her, for instance, the demand that she choose among options which offer nothing that she really wants.

Women want to define their identity. But they cannot do so by joining campaigns that do not bear directly on their own problems. That brings pseudo-liberation at the most. Women can only find their identity if the problems previously hidden in the private sphere are articulated and made into the focus for women's political solidarity and struggle. Most women are apolitical because the one-sided political parties have always ignored their needs. Women have tended to remain authoritarian in their demands for legal reform — because they have not recognized how subversive their demands really are.

Educated women with children are the easiest to politicize, for they are the most aggressive and articulate. These women, whom this society has given the opportunity to study, owe the privilege not to personal emancipation but to economic conditions. When these women have children, they are forced to play the roles from which they thought they were freed. Study must be interrupted or continued later; the demands made by husband and children retard or stop entirely this woman's intellectual growth. In addition, the woman feels insecure from having made no definite choice between blue stocking and housewife, between building a career at the cost of personal happiness or turning into a consumer-culture housewife. In other words, privileged women are the ones to realize that the middle class idea of emancipation is a lie, that they cannot liberate themselves by joining the general rat race, that the ethic of personal achievement has crippled them even in the midst of their privileged lives, and that the means used to win liberation decide the meaning of the word.

These women notice, at the very latest when they have children, that their privileges are entirely irrelevant. They are more than able to articulate the utter waste of the lives we lead — in other words, to bring the class struggle into their marriage. This means, objectively, that the husband becomes the exploiter or class enemy, which is, of course, a role he finds subjectively repugnant, since he has been forced into it by the achievement-oriented society.

These were the conclusions reached by the Action Council for Women's Liberation:

Women can neither liberate themselves as individuals nor wait for the revolution. A strictly political and economic revolution, in fact, does not end the repression characteristic of private life, as is obvious in any existing socialist country.

We are trying to achieve the sort of life in which competition between man and woman would cease. But this sort of democracy will be possible only when a change is made in the relations of production and the derivative power structure.

Since women with children, being the most victimized, are best prepared for solidarity and politicization, we have concentrated so far on their problems. We do not dismiss the difficulties of students without children; and we certainly see that, despite the universal oppression of women, class oppression also exists; but in order to be effective, we must start at a point where specific problems can be clearly and rationally analyzed.

We tried at first to bring up these conflicts in discussion with SDS members and at SDS meetings, but it was impossible. We withdrew and began working alone. That was six months ago, and most of our comrades laughed at us then. Today they complain that we shouldn't have dropped out. They try to tell us that, in general, we hold incorrect theories and they attribute to us nonsensical ideas which we have never believed, such as that women don't need men to be liberated. They insist — which we know — that they are oppressed too. But it's just that we've decided not to suffer helplessly the oppression they inflict on us because of their own oppression. It is exactly because we *do* think that liberation requires the cooperation of everyone that we are here today.

We must remind you once again that there are a few more women than men in this country. We think it's high time to make the demands and claims which our numbers merit, high time that these be met. If SDS finds it too difficult to follow this logic, then of course, we will be forced into a power struggle — something we would just as soon avoid. For us, it would be a waste of energy. We shall win, however, because our position is historically correct.

We don't enjoy being helpless and arrogant here today. We are helpless because we really expect progressive men to see that our fight is right. We are arrogant because we know how idiotically stubborn you are, not wanting to admit that people are organizing because you haven't organized them, and that there are so many people that if they were workers instead of women, you would greet it as the dawning of a better world.

Comrades, we're fed up with your games. You're plagued by hang-ups which you have to vent in aggression against women comrades who say something stupid or something you already know. That aggression is only partly explained as a political appraisal of the stupidity of your opponents. Why don't you admit that you are exhausted by this last year, that you don't know how you can stand the strain of dedicating yourselves physically and mentally to a cause which gives you no direct reward? Why don't you discuss, when you plan your programs, how on earth you intend to carry them out? Why do you all buy Wilhelm Reich? Why do you discuss the class struggle here and discuss at home what's lacking in your sex life? Isn't that a problem that can be discussed in SDS?

We don't accept or share your repressions.

This is what we have done in the isolation which we chose: we have concentrated on women with children, because they are the most victimized. Women with children can begin to think about themselves again only when their children's presence doesn't stand as a constant reminder of society's waste of human resources. Since politically minded women desperately want to keep their children out of a system of achievement and competition, we decided that for once we would be serious about society's demand that women raise their own children. We accepted this obligation in a special sense, by refusing to educate our children for competition and the pursuit of individual success. These, as we know, are the values which support capitalism.

We are trying to develop utopian models within existing society. And in them, our own needs will be recognized at last. Therefore, our concern with education is not a handy substitute for any desires we might have repressed for liberation. It is a necessary precondition for us to resolve our problems. Our hardest job is to avoid creating sheltered refuges for our children. We want to encourage them as they strive for freedom and so to give them the strength to face reality in a way that is committed to change.

Five of our Storefront Day Care Centers are in operation now; four more are in the process of being organized; others are in the early stages of planning. We are planning a Free University kindergarten and are organizing kindergarten teachers, or rather, helping them to organize themselves. As for theoretical work, we are working on a critique of the bourgeois conception of rationality and the patriarchal idea of objective or professional knowledge.

So many people are coming to us that we can hardly manage to organize them all. Our goal now is first to politicize the women who have some understanding of their problems. This will work best in the universities. But soon we must plan more generally applicable models in order to develop forms of collective education which do not just help the privileged. But we haven't got either the cadres or the knowledge for this. We cannot endanger our work by beginning ill-conceived projects in the workers' districts. The men who have come to us have been very eager to extend our work into workers' districts, but there are problems here.

First, many men have suddenly realized that something is happening that has some prospects. Having altered their vocabulary slightly, they have begun to dominate certain study groups, and the women, for the most part, cannot stop them. These men act as if they had invented the Day Care Centers; having grasped the political potential of the centers they tell the women not to bother with the problems of education. Their wish to use the centers to reach other population groups may well derive from the men's reluctance to articulate their own conflicts. For we have nothing to offer the workers now. We cannot take their children into our centers, where they would begin to behave in a way which would only get them into trouble at home. The conditions which would make it possible to give workers' children a different upbringing are yet to be created.

The centers will lead to more wide-ranging work. Children from the centers will not blend into the public school system and their parents will not tolerate those schools. We are trying to build, by organizing more centers, a broad base for the fight with the public schools. One can predict the sort of fight it will be by looking at some parents and children who did not go to our centers. We must not let our children learn only what capitalist society wants to teach them.

We are aware that meaningless jobs could be abolished. We are aware that we will need an enormous supply of teachers, male and female, for schools and kindergartens. There is no reason why 90 percent of all female workers should be unskilled. Comrades, you can see that we orient our work differently:

1. We have limited ourselves to education and areas relevant to it.
2. All our funds go to the centers and work connected with them.
3. We are taking the time to prepare for our next task, and for the politicization of private life.
4. If we think that the centers are a feasible experiment, we will move on to the schools.
5. Besides this, of course, we are doing theoretical work, which involves placing our ideas in a wider intellectual context.

If SDS is an organization of people who want to stimulate liberating processes in order to make revolution possible, then SDS must recognize our work and draw some conclusions.

This brings us to the matter of priorities.

We must discuss: Should some groups concentrate on students in the trade schools and begin to organize them, or should we concentrate on developing preschool organizations for a wider range of groups?

Organizing in the vocational schools will catch the few, privileged male graduates of the public elementary schools who managed to continue their education, however bad that education is. Organizing students in higher education will catch the few privileged and advanced students who happen to have liberal parents prepared to support them in school. The leaders of such organizations always have preconceptions which accept the educational system, preconceptions which the schools instilled. But we want to erase those preconceptions. Should we build some organization to fight NATO and the military, or should we concentrate on the social classes which the ruling class absolutely must manipulate in order to perpetuate itself?

Comrades, if you are not ready for serious discussion, we must conclude that SDS is full of nothing more than counter-revolutionary hot air.

In that case, the women of our organization will know what to do.

Manifesto of the Action Council of Women's Liberation

We, the Action Council of Women's Liberation, are a *political group.* We belong to the party of those who fight repression and authoritarianism and we work in cooperation with the various groups of the APO.

We are concerned with the oppression of women in our society but we are *not a bourgeois women's liberation movement.* We do not view the problems of women as a matter of individual conditioning and we do not restrict ourselves to court battles for equal rights or applications for state aid. In short, we disassociate ourselves from every reform movement which lacks a firm commitment to attack the economic and social foundations of our competitive capitalist system.

Hence we do not want "equal rights for women," which would mean, essentially, that they get a fair chance in economic and social competition with men. Rather, we want a life without competition among human beings. We think that this can be achieved only by transforming the economic structure of society and the distribution of power by means of an economic and social revolution which would create a *socialist society.*

The fact that we realize that abolishing the oppression of women presupposes a socialist revolution does not mean that we intend to wait for a revolution. The progress made in socialist countries has proved that our main problems, which concern particularly repression in private life and the separation of private and public realms, cannot be solved by economic and social change alone. We must therefore begin to work on our problems now.

As socialist countries have failed to solve our specific problems, so have those groups which consider themselves to be the socialist avant-garde of our country (SDS). For just as men have always been the chief instigators of socialist changes, so men have always set the policies of these progressive groups, and we view them as privileged. Hence it seems clear to us that the work now before Women's Liberation must be done largely *without the cooperation of men.*

Our conclusions do not constitute a claim that women do not need men in order to achieve liberation. Our withdrawal is only temporary, so that we can be in a position to define ourselves without consideration for and compromises with men. Only then shall we be able to work cooperatively and productively with other groups. Let us remember the French students: Only when a group has become conscious of its *own* problems and fought with all its might for its *own* interests can that group catalyze other groups and initiate the transformation of society.

Action Council for Women's Liberation, West Berlin Chapter, Berlin
October 16, 1968

NOTES ON A MEETING OF THE ACTION COUNCIL'S
TASK FORCE ON LIBERATION

Meeting of June 6, 1968

Reports on nonrepressive schools: A. S. Neill (Summerhill) and Vera Schmidt (Moscow Child Care Laboratory)

We cannot wholeheartedly support such experiments for three reasons:

1. Such insulated schools, as long as the society outside remains bourgeois and authoritarian, can only fail, for when the children leave the school, they would either (a) feel engulfed by society and compelled to adjust, in which case their education was sheer waste, or (b) because of the sort of character formed by nonrepressive education, they would be unable to compromise with the world they found; and having been thus forced into total self-reliance their ego-strength would decline or they might become neurotic, even psychotic. In that case, it would be better had they gone to an ordinary authoritarian school.

2. Since, at least to our knowledge, no comprehensive *follow-up* has ever been done on children from Summerhill or the Child Care Laboratory, we cannot know whether our suspicions are justified.

3. Such nonrepressive schools, scattered enclaves against an entire culture, although they may have some short-term influence on bourgeois society, can have little long-term effect. Only in a socialist society, and only after giving an identical education to many generations of boys and girls, would it be possible to eliminate phylogenetic factors in the male and female personalities and to find out exactly what effect gender has on character. A cross-cultural, historical study of all children — which could well be impossible — would take a lifetime, and given the gargantuan task of wading through the data, one wonders if the findings of a strictly comparative study would be worth it.

We found another problem when we tried to acquaint ourselves, at least superficially, with the mechanisms of child rearing as it is practiced in our society. The studies that did exist on education and personality development concerned boys; practically no comprehensive research had been done on small girls. In most studies, the word "child" was a synonym for "boy."

Though still concerned with childhood development, we decided to stop focussing on the concept of "education." The related concepts of marriage and family, which are now our major concerns, seemed equally central to an understanding of the position and image of women in bourgeois society.

To avoid having to make empty generalizations about an unmanageably broad subject, we tried to define a limited area on which we could concentrate with some hope of perceptible results — results useful for a better understanding of women's emancipation. Since we want to understand how bourgeois society conceptualizes "woman," it seems most fruitful to study the image and role of women in a situation in which the principles of capitalism had been carried to their logical conclusion — fascism. (Reading: "Authority and Family" in Wilhelm Reich, *The Mass Psychology of Fascism*, Noonday, 1970.)

THE MEETING OF THE WOMEN'S TASK FORCE ON EDUCATION
WHICH LED TO THE FOUNDING OF THE
FIRST CHARLOTTENBURG STOREFRONT DAY CARE CENTER

Notes — Meeting of April 2, 1968

Our last meeting had the highest attendance so far (about 25) and several newcomers. A short report was given on Vera Schmidt's "Model of Non-repressive Education." There was hardly any real discussion of this Moscow experiment of 1921–1924. It became clear that we should not begin with Vera Schmidt, because even to evaluate the relevance of her project to our plans would require special knowledge and a special point of view. We felt that we needed to agree on some other specific reading. We considered three areas as essential preliminaries to studying the literature on child raising and education: (1) psychoanalysis and sexuality, e.g., the work of Wilhelm Reich, (2) anthropology, Margaret Mead, and (3) works by Marxist authors on marriage and family, for example, Marx and Engels, *Origins of the Family*.

We decided to read first Wilhelm Reich's book *The Sexual Revolution*. Clearly, everyone was very interested in the subject of sexuality; no one argued that it didn't have an important connection with child raising. There was no such general agreement on the necessity of relating sexuality and psychoanalytic concepts, taken broadly, to an analysis of the whole society. Two books were suggested: Wilhelm Reich, *Psychoanalysis and Dialectical Materialism*, and Herbert Marcuse, *Eros and Civilization*.

The discussion showed, as had the previous ones, that we still neither shared a philosophy defining our goals and methods of work nor agreed on how theory should be applied to the problems we face in developing a kindergarten.

We did agree that goal-directedness was imperative; and we must decide exactly what results we want and select the means to achieve them. In other words, we thought that we should study child education only as it applies to the system which we wish to destroy and the one we want to build.

As for a concrete educational model — some kind of working utopia — we thought that it must, in theory and in actuality, be a tool of the political struggle. This whole idea is complex and raises innumerable problems and we have only begun to discuss them. The "Introduction to Vera Schmidt" pamphlet (see "Documents" above, pp. 16 ff.) was recommended as a stimulus to discussion.

PEOPLE WORKING IN SOCIALIST DAY CARE CENTERS — MEET
SUNDAY EVENING, NOVEMBER 25, 9 P.M., AT
THE TECHNICAL UNIVERSITY! ! ! !

If we don't know something, we should admit it, not pretend we do . . . that's why we shall take up the suggestion often made in the Central Council of the

Day Care Centers and have a general open meeting. Everybody who wants to work in a socialist way on or in the centers should come.

Before the general meeting, all study groups and task forces of the Action Council of Women's Liberation will hold meetings in the Technical University, beginning Saturday the 23rd at 9 o'clock to lay out our many problems for the large general discussion.

At the general meeting we must outline a program that implements our educational philosophy. This should lead each Center to prepare a report which will be heard and discussed at another meeting two or three days later.

The two Charlottenburg centers have made some suggestions for conducting the meeting, which hopefully are being discussed and improved in the different centers between now and Saturday. We think that *only careful preparation by each participating group can lead to a productive general discussion.* Everyone is to study the points carefully, discuss them socialistically within each Center, and *be absolutely sure to come Saturday!*

Enter at June 17th Street. Signs will be posted on room numbers.

1. *Why don't we want our children to go to public kindergartens?*
   a. What experiences have parents had with public kindergartens?
   b. What experiences have teachers now working with us had with public kindergartens?
   c. Statistics on West Berlin kindergartens.
2. *Reports of the individual centers*
   a. Organizational Matters
      Size of rooms/furniture/schedule/getting the children to and from school/outings/playgrounds/space problems/division of manual and theoretical labor.
   b. Finances
      Calculation of upkeep costs/negotiations with the Senate/ideas on fund raising/lists of possible contributors/pooling resources.
   c. Working with the Parents
      Meeting: how often and where?/main factors in communication/organizing parental discussions on children/parent-child relationships/family situations/financial problems of members.
   d. Communication Among Parents Beyond the Minimum of Required Work
      Forming study groups/developing projects/changing family situations/common housing/communes/psychoanalytic groups/working with groups from the Technical University or the Free University.
   e. Situation of Women in the Centers

Starting point: the Action Council/relationship between the Centers and the Action Council/women working cooperatively in the Centers/ has their situation within their family changed?/division of labor/situation of men.

   g. Childhood Development

Which methods produce which educational results?/ways of keeping written notes on children and discussing them/what new possibilities have opened up in the children's lives which they lacked before?/ effects of the group on the individual child/is a children's collective forming?/play situations/what kinds of play should be deliberately encouraged?/how?/how is sexuality expressed and transformed?/ Eating: how?/what?/cleanliness.

   h. Relationship of the Centers to the Action Council of Women's Liberation

Cooperation/how can the Council help to resolve conflicts?

  3. *The centers and their political significance*

   a. Function in the present system/the concept of a model of the counter-culture/how can our experiment bring out the contradictions of the system?/how can these contradictions activate the centers?/participating with the children in demonstrations/campaigns and actions initiated by the centers/and by the centers in collaboration with the Action Council of Women's Liberation.

If you really care about the kids, and if as a woman you want to change your terrible situation concerning the family+child+husband's money trap, don't make excuses — come! Partial cooperation between the two Charlottenburg Centers has shown that specific situations, even if one hasn't directly experienced them, can be shared and understood. Since different centers began at different times, it will be interesting to work out the first results and the special problems of each group.

Charlottenburg I and II
VENCEREMOS

Saturday   23 November   9 o'clock at the June 17th Street entrance

**ACTION COUNCIL FOR WOMEN'S LIBERATION —
STUDY GROUP ON THE THEORY OF EMANCIPATION**
Reading Plan (from October 3, 1968)
Unit I: Critical theory and liberation
  — Adorno: *Sexual Taboos and Law*
  — Adorno: *Minima Moralia*

— Adorno and Horkheimer: *Dialectric of Enlightenment,* especially "Man and Animal"

— Horkheimer: *Theoretical Sketches on Authority and the Family*

— Fromm: Social-psychological chapters in above

Unit II: Fascism and Femininity

— Wilhelm Reich: *The Mass Psychology of Fascism*

— reports on: Alfred Rosenberg, *The Myth of the Twentieth Century*, and Anna Maria Herbst, *Political Ideologies and the Political Role of Women* (example of a fascist book on women written by a woman)

Unit III: Freud on Female Sexuality — three essays:

— "On cultural sexual morality and modern neurosis"

— "Some psychological consequences of the anatomical sex differences"

— "On female sexuality"

As a necessary connection between Units III and IV:

— Engels: *The Origin of the Family, Private Property, and the State*

Unit IV: Socialist Psychoanalysis; The Sexual Politics Movement

— Wilhelm Reich: *The Collapse of Sexual Morality*
                   The Function of the Orgasm

— reports on: the history of the sexual politics movement, sexual legislation in Russia after 1917, the controversy in Lenin's writings on sexual freedom

Unit V: Sociological and Psychological Material on Marriage and the Family, Child Rearing, Childhood, and Woman (ample bibliographies in libraries)

— Rene Spitz and W. Godfrey Cobliner: *The First Year of Life*

— Anna Freud, Sandor Ferenczi, S. Bernfeld, and Övermann are some useful names.

Unit VI: Woman as Spouse

— August Bebel: *Woman and Socialism* (1879)

— Lenin: *Call to Working Women*

— Clara Zotkin: *Forward!*

— Clara Zotkin: *Lenin's Legacy to the Women of the World*

— Otto Ruhle: *The Socialization of Women*

— Mao Tse-Tung: *Quotations from Chairman Mao Tse-Tung,* "On Contradiction"

Unit VII: (to be planned) Utopia and Liberation

A further bibliography in the fall of 1968 adds the following authors to the list:

— Nelly Wolfheim: Essays in *Imago*

— Gustav Bally: *Introduction to the Psychoanalytic Theory of Freud*

— Zulliger: *Fear of Our Children*

— Aichorn: (popular contemporary German writer, like Zulliger)

— Otto Ruhle: *The Spirit of Proletarian Children*
— E. Richter: *Parents, Children, and Neurosis*
— Bittner/Rehm: *Psychoanalysis and Education*
— H. Kentler: *Revision of Sexual Education*
— Siegfried Bernfeld: *Sisyphus or the Limits of Education*
— Bronislaw Malinowski: *Sex and Repression in Savage Society*
— Margaret Mead
— Alexander Mitscherlich: *Society Without the Father*
— Peter Furstenau: *Sociology of Child Rearing*
— Reimut Reiche: *Sexuality and the Class Struggle*

2. Collective Child Raising — Planning and Opening the First Centers

The Women's Liberation Action Council began in January 1968 with certain women, active SDS members, who became aware of the discrepancy between the revolutionary demand for "a transformation of human relationships" and the actual position of women in the movement.

The antiauthoritarian protest of SDS and its sympathizers was aimed at every form of oppression, "believing that only marginal groups, intellectuals, and privileged elements on the fringe of the system could represent the working class and, in some sense, regardless of class differences, initiate a revolution for humanity" (H. Krahl, RPK, no. 53, 20.2.1970).

The fact that at this stage in the movement many specific groups of oppressed people began organizing came out of the idea that

to fight this society, we must begin, in the very way we conduct the political struggle, to sow the first seeds. To provide the first models for an alternate approach to human relationships, one freed from the duality of oppressor and oppressed. . . . To deny this society and catalyze another pattern of relationships, we must be able, as individuals, to renounce our own egoism for the sake of the freedom of others and, at least partially, to repress ourselves to ensure that freedom for each individual coincides with freedom for others.

What Comrade Krahl pleads for so eloquently here worked out somewhat differently in reality. Women learned from discussions and demonstrations. At demonstrations they fought as bravely as the men, but when the time came for planning or criticizing actions, they found that they simply didn't get a chance to speak; the leaders of SDS discussions silenced women just as effectively as the leaders of university seminars. Moreover, mothers could not voice their protest in the liberating activity of demonstrating. They pushed their carriages alongside the march or behind the front ranks, or else hauled their toddlers along for miles. Frequently, they were insulted for doing even this. The alternative was to stay home as passive sympathizers in the movement and to admire, or nurse, the heroes on their return. This hit hardest the wives and girl friends of men in the movement.

Through the Vietnam conference, which put the spotlight on SDS solidarity with liberation struggles in the third world, many women became more conscious of their chains. They felt that only by fighting their own oppression could they express any real solidarity with the third world. But finding a strategy was still a problem, for guns would be of little use to the women in this battle.

So there were two factors that motivated the first women's liberation cell: (1) recognition of the need for a revolutionary transformation of society through political struggle and of the woman's special role in that struggle; and (2) the woman's subordinate role in what was supposed to be a struggle for universal liberation.

This second realization obliged the women to direct their protest first against their own comrades, men with whom they had previously fought side by side, as fellow student, colleague, friend, or wife. . . . They organized now with other women, strove for some comprehension of their own situation, and tried to work out a political strategy to reach the doubly oppressed women of the underprivileged classes. Since arrogant male comrades interrupted the whole effort time and time again, the Action Group banned men from discussions and deliberately separated itself from the SDS organization.

At first, SDS treated the women's actions with good-natured ridicule. The standard male line was to tell the wife or girl friend, "Go out and liberate yourself a little." There was no interest in the Action Group's work. This was precisely the response which earlier efforts in women's liberation had elicited, an attitude now rationalized by talk about "lack of political relevance." In the fall of 1968, however, when a woman read a resolution of the Action Group before the Congress of SDS representatives in Frankfurt and a few tomatoes got thrown, the male attitude began to shift. They suddenly discovered that the Day Care Centers, the concrete product of the Action Group's work, were politically significant.

Founding of the First Day Care Centers

Even in the Action Group's very first political discussion, it was observed that women with small children were definitely handicapped. Solving this problem was the first priority.

The results of meetings on this subject appeared in a flyer, distributed to female students at the Free University of West Berlin:

The broad repression characteristic of society bears down hardest on women, who in turn vent the aggression received from society on their children. Largely due to lack of time, women are in no position to reflect upon their situation and draw the logical conclusions. Even the organizations which want equal participation by women have only a small number of female members, usually, as individuals, less productive than the men. . . . There is an acute need for some organization which would relieve mothers, at scheduled times, from the burden of caring for their children so that they could do political work. The major reasons for the frustration of this need are:

(a) the shortage of kindergartens and

(b) the authoritarian practices of existing kindergartens, which makes sending children to them tantamount to damaging healthy growth.

The conclusion is obvious: we must immediately found our own kindergartens.

The flyer invited all women to an open meeting at the Free University. Around 80 appeared and about half had children. Not all were students; because of their children, many had dropped out of school and were working part time or at home. After considerable discussion it was agreed to begin by forming groups in every major district in the city to work out plans for a kindergarten. It was suggested that, until such a kindergarten actually opened, all the children could come to the home of one member and there be taken care of by the various parents in turn. The Action Group agreed to coordinate this project and to keep a file of those interested in participating.

The group arranged to have their next meeting at the Republican Club.

Even at this first meeting, the difficulties one might expect in such a self-help project came up and practical problems soon became apparent. Not all homes could serve as the place for a large number of children to play for several hours. Some children did not want to leave their mothers and frequent changes of environment made them fearful or aggressive. The parents who happened to have the most suitable house often suffered an intolerable amount of pressure. We also noticed that the children reacted differently to the various supervising parents, and that a child who had a parent present would usually be too jealous of that parent to be able to take part in play. Only certain parents, moreover, could competently care for many children for a relatively long period. These problems showed us that we had to find a suitable place for the children quickly, a place which would become familiar and where there would be no inhibitions due to concern for the possessions of adults. It also seemed necessary that the parents meet at least weekly for a thorough discussion of the problems of child rearing as well as organizational difficulties.

The Action Council suggested the creation of different study groups which would systematically collect literature and discuss the problems of psychological liberation and child raising. The women working in the various kindergarten projects could also participate in these study groups. The findings would be brought to the parents' weekly meetings and, eventually, be put in writing and made generally available. The political goal was to make possible self-organization in the business of child raising for other, less privileged groups. We were aware, however, of our need to gain some experience first.

When the groups started looking for buildings, it became clear that because landlords feared disturbing their other tenants, ordinary residences had to be ruled out. But we also noticed that almost every district possessed vacant stores, small businesses ruined by the self-service chains. The Neuköln group rented the first store in February, and from then on, we named our kindergartens "Storefront Day Care Centers." A little later, two more centers sprang up in Schöneberg (cf. documents recording the founding of the first Schöneberg Center).

A Nonauthoritarian Program of Child Raising

The Charlottenburg group was the first Day Care Center to formulate its concepts of collective child raising in a provisional set of policies.

This group had organized at the first meeting with the Action Group in February. After some preliminary talks, five couples (mainly artists and students) agreed to develop the Day Care Center through comprehensive discussion of child raising in a parents' study group. They began by reading A. S. Neill's *Summerhill*, about the free school which is usually considered to be the only ongoing attempt at nonrepressive education. Though the group agreed in general with Neill's ideas on noncoercive learning and collective living, no one could quite accept his élitism, which makes this type of education available only to the upper middle class. The school was criticized for being a "liberated island for the fortunate" — a refuge in the midst of a repressive, exploitative society open only to those with enough money. Since Neill never presented the wider social context which his educational theory implies — in fact, since he consciously avoided doing so — his model seemed absolutely worthless as a step towards revolution.

The study group then concentrated on Marxist authors who, working from the concept of a socialist transformation of society, criticized capitalism's methods of child raising and proposed alternate approaches (Marx, Engels, Reich, Vera Schmidt; cf. document recording this group's discussions, pp. 16 ff.).

At the end of April, Commune 2 joined this group. Commune 2 had already experienced the disjunction between public kindergarten and their own approach to collective life. Of this problem, they wrote:

In important ways, the children had much more scope in unrestricted free play than is allowed in the bourgeois family. We tried, as much as possible, not to influence their play and not to force store-bought toys and storytelling on them. A playroom crammed with "toys" corresponds to prohibiting the use of objects appropriated from the adult world in games. In the commune, the children had a great deal of freedom to play with furniture and supplies from the adult world (mattresses, chairs, tables, dishes). It seems important to us, if play is to succeed as a way of mastering reality, that the objects from that

*threatening adult world are precisely those which should be
stripped of their fixed function and given a new one in play
(e.g., chairs lined up to make a train). At meals, we did not
force the children to eat at all or to empty their plates. Although
it earned us the contempt of the public kindergarten teachers,
we preferred to let them wear dirty clothes if they wanted.
A child's love for an item of clothing seemed more important
to us than the coercive social demand for immaculateness.
Until fall, we bathed the children almost every night. This
didn't mean limiting them to an official cleaning up; cleanliness
was just a byproduct of all the joyful activity the children put
into bathing. Only in the mornings, before they went to kindergarten, did we methodically wash their faces and hands.*

— Commune 2, *Attempt to Revolutionize Bourgeois
Individuals*, Berlin, 1960, pp. 80 f.

We tried not to curb the self-expression of the children by
constant prohibitions and aggression, even when their actions
did not coincide with our preconceptions of cleanliness and
order. At first, we ran the risk of using manipulation to overcome
the children's resistance to certain of our demands. Liberal
parents, hesitant about using overt prohibitions or force, com-
monly apply this kind of insidious pressure. Such behavior
obscures, for the child, the objective clash between his wishes
and parental demands. Thus the child cannot direct aggression
against the cause of his frustration, but must seek other targets.
This is the kind of education that tends to produce nondirected
or masochistic aggression, evidenced in incessant grumbling
and whining.

In our discussions, we soon recognized our tendency to
manipulative evasion of the children's demands. We therefore
undertook, when prohibitions seemed unavoidable, to voice
and justify them clearly, rather than deviously preventing the
children from doing certain things, like using the record player
on their own or playing in the study (ibid., p. 78).

The Commune children had repeatedly refused to go to the
public kindergarten, and the Communards thought they might
begin taking the center children on outings during the weekends,
to get some experience even while the Day Care Center was
still in the planning stage. This would get the children and the
parents acquainted and put the theoretical preparation to a
practical test. Commune 2 observed about these outings:

Most children only wanted to go if at least one of their parents came along. At first, therefore, the parents did come to help the children adjust to the novelty. . . . After a few weeks most of the children were no longer afraid; only the two- and three-year-olds and a few of the older children insisted on the presence of their parents. The Commune children had no problems in this regard. In the weekly center parents' meeting, we had, from the beginning, proposed finding a "neutral" person who would regularly take out the children and eventually work in the Day Care Center. . . . The outings confirmed our opinion. Those children whose parents always came along had the most problems: they were the most aggressive; they needed constant reassurance about their mother or father; sometimes they could not tolerate other children asking their parents for help, and would then have trouble playing with the others; usually, they were trying in some way to show off for their parents.

The situation was new for the parents, too. They had difficulty in behaving as usual towards their own children and often assumed a forced neutrality, attempting to treat their child just like one of the group. This, of course, intensified the fears of their own child. About a month after the outings began, we found a kindergarten teacher who has remained with the children. She had quit her job in the public kindergarten because conditions there forced her into a police role. She worked with the parents to plan a physical layout for our center more conducive to the growth of freedom and initiative (ibid., pp. 96 f.).

During this period, there were weekly planning meetings for the proposed Storefront Day Care Center. Before presenting the final program which came out of these meetings, we wish to briefly outline the psychoanalytic theory of early childhood, the basis of the program. We are going to draw on "Socialization and Compensatory Ways of Raising Children," the collective effort of students from the Sociology Seminar at the Free University of West Berlin, which one participant brought to our weekly discussions.

Personality Development in Early Childhood

The Oral Stage (first year of life)
Sigmund Freud saw in the sucking of the nursing infant "the three fundamental characteristics of infantile sexuality. This sexuality originates in connection with a vital physiological func-

tion; it is autoerotic, lacking a sexual object; and its sexual purpose
is determined by an erogenous zone." René Spitz distinguished
three steps in the formation of libido objects:

1. the objectless or preobject stage,
2. the stage of recognition of an object and desire for that object,
3. the stage of libido fixation on another human being.

Objectless stage (primary narcissism). There is as yet no perception, in the sense of recognition of environmental stimuli; only
internal stimuli (tactile experience, nurture, circulation, and
breathing) elicit responses, although the infant is not conscious of
giving these responses. Survival requires the development of
perception, which enables the infant to recognize and to take
nourishment from the environment. "All perception begins in the
oral cavity, the original bridge between internal and external
perception" (Spitz). "Hand, ear and skin are auxiliary organs in
perception, and, in this stage, are subordinated to the oral cavity.
The unity of need-satisfaction and perception is the precondition
for the development of initial memory imprints."

The stage at which an object is recognized and desired occurs
in the third month, when the primary form of tactile contact
perception (of the nipple) is supplemented by the perception of a
more distant face, which remains constant even though the nipple
is repeatedly lost. With his first smile in response to this human
face, the infant shifts from responding to internal stimuli to per-
ceiving external ones. As he invests external stimuli with libidinal
energy, the infant necessarily breaks through the immediate and
unconditioned functioning of the pleasure-pain principle. The
distinction between conscious, preconscious, and unconscious
mind becomes possible. Ego and id are separated; the operations
of the rudimentary ego begin.

The stage of fixing the libido on a human object begins when
"eighth month anxiety" appears: the child shows fear in the presence of strangers because he thinks his mother has gone away.
The mother, the only focus for the libido, is now not only a visual
but also an emotional object. The child's psychic organization now
permits goal-directed expression of feelings. The basic trust of the
child in the mother has been established; this, according to
Erikson, is necessary for any further psychic development.

Pathologies of the oral phase. Besides weaning, long known to be a traumatic experience, we now understand, through Spitz's studies, the concept of affective, especially tactile, deprivation. This is the way in which the child's development tends to reflect the mother's problems with her surroundings. Unsatisfactory relationships in the mother's life, guilt about the existence of the infant and its sexual character, tend to provoke in the mother various expressions of resistance to her own repressed instincts.

In early infancy, open rejection by the mother produces unconsciousness in the infant: up to the third month, overanxious solicitude produces colic; hostility expressed in nervousness leads to skin eczemas; frequent oscillations between hostility and reconciliation result in hyperactivity. Partial, or even total, lack of affection leads to dullness, stagnation, and even regression. Institutionalized orphans, without a mother or substitute to provide maternal care, have been shown to develop at a rate which, in the second year of life, was 45 percent below average, thus putting the child at the level of idiocy. Normal children, separated from the mother after some months of a satisfying relationship, showed similar results. . . . If the mother did not return after a few months, the pathological effect became the same as for the foundlings — irreversible illness due to institutionalization. Spitz, who observed these children to age four, reports that they could not sit, stand, walk, or speak. Of 91 children observed in an orphanage, 34 had died before the age of two.
— "Socialization and Compensatory Ways of Raising Children,"
MS. Berlin, 1969, pp. 16 f.

Pedagogical conclusions. According to Mitscherlich, in the first year it is impossible to spoil an infant. The infant has the right to demand everything and give nothing. During this time, the demand-feeding system is right, and one should freely and promptly satisfy every wish. This means: no fixed nursing schedule, no premature weaning, no allowing the baby to cry through the night, no attempts at toilet training, serene and consistent treatment in the early period, ample tactile contact, and rocking. The infant should be able to let himself go, practically without concern. After a time, stimuli to encourage grasping, turning, etc., may be tried. Then the child will begin to live in an extroverted way and to develop a basic trust (Erikson), essential to the later manifestation of an exploratory spirit.

Anal Stage of Development

After age one, infantile sexuality enters the anal-sadistic stage. Freud connects the predominance of sadistic and anal impulses with the appearance of teeth, muscular strengthening, and growing control of anal and urethral sphincters. Erogenous investment is almost completely transferred from the oral mucous membranes to the anal zone. The simple autoerotic pleasure of pressing and forcing, sensing the fecal mass, and exercising the sphincter is partly transformed, through the child's active interest in his own excrement, into a kind of object-love (Ferenczi). Apparently, the contents of the colon are considered part of the body, the first "product" that the child can "give away." The child can express his feelings of fitting in with the environment by expulsion of his feces, his opposition by retention.

At this stage, both passive tendencies (especially those directed towards the erogenous membranes) and active ones are present; later, in the genital stage, these will become female and male traits (Freud). Erikson assumes an alternation between tension and relaxation. The anal zone is particularly suited to express the stubborn insistence on one's own impulses by willful retention of feces, as opposed to giving them up. At the same time, muscular development enables the child to grasp and hold objects or to throw and kick them away, to hold things close or at a distance — in short, to increasingly master his surroundings. This whole phase engages the child in a fight for autonomy.

The child's capacity to make his will known, generally by holding on or letting go (Erikson), inevitably conflicts with adult demands. In our culture the child's struggle for autonomy and parental expectations clash, particularly over the matter of toilet training, which has a decisive influence on the resolution of the entire anal stage. Premature or excessively strict toilet training, accompanied by fear of punishment, buffets the child between demands that he empty his bowels and, at other times, that he not empty them. He cannot learn gradually, according to his own will, to master his sphincter muscles and control his other natural functions. For him this involves a double rebellion and a double defeat. To reestablish his balance, he must either regress to the oral stage or develop, in defense, reaction-formations (stubbornness, hostility).

Pathology of the anal stage. Contrary to Freud's belief, intense and constant interest in the anal zone and feces is not a natural result of the anal phase; rather it characterizes those children whose relationship with the mother is already troubled (as is, unfortunately, frequently the case). The normal significance of this stage lies in the growth of object relations, essential for the full development of the child's capacities (not only muscular coordination, but, in particular, the ability to recognize objects, to talk, to initiate and manipulate contact with other human beings).

If this development is stunted, it makes relations with the environment and the discovery of new things very difficult. The personality is limited in its potential and later appears rigid (fixed, immovable, stern). The coercive or anal character, with its familiar traits of stinginess, excessive cleanliness, stubbornness, is a pathological exaggeration of this rigidity.

Pedagogical conclusions. Let toilet training be forgotten. Interest in the anal processes should be encouraged, never suppressed. Although play with feces should not be forbidden, substitutes (sand and water, clay, finger paints) can be introduced gradually. Training should begin only when: 1) the child can sit up alone, 2) can control his sphincter, and 3) can make his needs known. The transition from potty to toilet should be made only at the child's wish. Adults must try to minimize and silence their acquired disgust.

The Infantile-Genital or Phallic Stage of Development

Around two or three-and-a-half, the genital stage begins. Freud named it the phallic stage after the male genital to emphasize that, in this stage, the female pleasure drive, oriented to the clitoris, the embryonic equivalent of the penis, is equally phallic. Although penis and clitoris masturbation are the dominant forms of sexual activity, there is also pleasure in voyeuristic, exhibitionist, and anal or urethral erotic activities. At this stage, a powerful and intense sexual curiosity appears; its suppression or inhibition leads to a decline in curiosity in general and to a loss of intellectual potential. Masturbation, an activity needed to discharge the built-up libidinal tension, will involve incestuous fantasies. The child will overtly try to seduce his parents, persons who take care of him, and his brothers and sisters. These attempts meet both direct and indirect prohibitions by adults and so form the basis for the Oedipal conflict.

The male Oedipus complex. As early as the late oral stage, the boy develops an object-love for his mother, which begins with breast contact and is later strengthened. He develops toward the father a sense of identification, the wish to become like him. Although less intense than toward the nurturing mother, there is object-love for the father. Both relationships coexist peacefully until the development of genital sexuality adds a new dimension to love for the mother and creates hate and death-wishes toward the father, who obstructs this love relationship. Since positive object-love for the father continues simultaneously, the relationship to him becomes ambivalent. Thus the simple Oedipus complex in a boy can be defined as mixed emotions towards the father and a purely positive object-love towards the mother.

Sexual relations with the mother are expressed in bodily contact and, indirectly, in the desire to have the mother masturbate the child, a wish which dominates intense fantasies during masturbation. Both strivings are limited by various sanctions, which can be grouped under the general heading of castration threats. These produce "castration anxiety" in the boy, and, according to Freud, this intolerable anxiety eventually leads him to renounce the mother and end the Oedipus complex.

Castration anxiety has several sources. One is the threat of castration as a punishment for masturbation and for a conscious or unconscious preoccupation with the genitals. The threat may be overtly expressed or conveyed simply through an antisexual atmosphere. The threat can also be transferred to symbolic equivalents such as eyes, fingers, and hands. The second important aspect of this threat is the discovery that girls lack a penis, which Freud terms the gravest trauma in a boy's life. To save his "intensely loved" penis, incestuous wishes are now almost violently put aside. This is achieved by means of a new element in the psyche, the so-called superego.

The female Oedipus complex. Since the girl, like the boy, took the mother as a love-object in the earlier stages, she now focuses her sexuality on her as strongly as the boy does. Prohibitions, spoken or unspoken, about incest and masturbation make girls, too, feel a great deal of tension. The boy overcomes his Oedipus complex by seeing the female genitals. Usually the girl cannot accept the lack of a penis and blames her mother for it. Her feelings of penis envy at first lead to a desire for the father's penis and then to the wish to have a child by the father. This marks the end of the girl's infantile development. Since the girl's close ties with her mother normally cause a strong identification with her, she accepts the same love-object, the father. While in the boy castration fears end the complex, the anxieties engendered by the girl's belief that she has already been castrated are what actually produce her Oedipus complex. Since the girl does not undergo the chief experience leading to the resolution of the Oedipus complex, she retains this complex for an indeterminate time, gradually, and only partially, to relinquish it in later life. The female superego, therefore, does not usually become as powerful as the male's.

Oedipus complex and superego. The superego is the part of the psyche that controls the expression of unconscious drives in conscious action according to certain moral prescriptions. It develops through identification: loss of the love-object is compensated for by taking over, "internalizing," certain of its parts, namely character traits and concepts of value. But this by no means explains why the self-hating Oedipal boy identifies with the father, the very person toward whom he has negative feelings.

A result of renunciation is more or less complete identification with the object which forces one to it. It seems paradoxical, but such are the unalterable facts: we become similar in character to the figure we have to hate because we are not allowed to love him. The fundamental drive which here serves to cause identification is love, but the stimulus to identification is the hatred produced by a painful renunciation: thus the object that one could not stop loving and that one had to hate because it would give no satisfaction, becomes the model for character formation of the ego and ego-ideal.

— Wilhelm Reich

Pathology of the infantile-genital stage. There are many infantile neuroses. During the very period in which active attempts at possession as a means of developing autonomous social capacities must be evidenced, the child, because of numerous and virtually insurmountable anxieties, cannot make any such efforts. Fear of sleep, fear that those adults who take care of him will leave, fear of the dark, nightmares, bed wetting, etc., are typical. Animals are the most common fear. (Boys usually fear large animals, which might bite or eat them; girls usually fear insects, mice, and snakes, which might enter and damage their bodies.) In this way, fear of punishment for sexual activity, although displaced to an external object, continues. If the child accumulates such displacements, the external world can become such a dangerous place that the armor of anxiety-reactions needed to face it greatly diminishes the scope of potential actions and generally inhibits development.

A later transcendence of childhood fears does not supply in itself a cure for the illness. The majority of people feel powerless and crave leadership; this sheeplike man is a product of overly repressive ways of raising children, those exact ways which meet the needs of an authoritarian-capitalist society. At this point, psychology, with its orientation to the individual, moves into a socioeconomic perspective. For repressive ways of raising children cannot really be attributed solely to a parental superego, since that superego itself is only a reflection of the systematic mutilation of humanity by man's continuing exploitation of man in the interest of capital.

Pedagogical conclusions. For the genital stage it isn't possible, as with the other stages, simply to give some tips on behavior, for the conflicts here are the inevitable outcome of the father-mother-child nuclear family structure. Therefore, they cannot be mitigated within the family.

Whether parents are lenient or strict with the child is not important, for the child's character is influenced far more by the family structure than by the father's conscious aims and methods. Considering his power, even his kindliness . . . , seems less a matter of natural behavior than of magnanimity conferring a debt . . . any measure taken in raising children, be it ever so sensible, must smack of the basic alternatives: candy and beatings.
— Horkheimer, *Studies on Authority and the Family*, 1936, p. 59

Later we will discuss how parents and children in collectives can, to some extent, mitigate this conflict. Since all adults have presumably been subjected to repressive training, their behavior will certainly be strongly influenced by their own repressions, unconscious fears, and feelings of guilt and disgust.

Conditions Determining Character Formation

The development of character serves the immediate purpose of strengthening the ego and reducing the pressure of repressed feelings. The ego identifies itself with the reality that blocks wish fulfillment, initially, with the person who is the chief obstacle to that fulfillment. The ego then turns against itself the aggressions originally directed against that particular person. This results in a simultaneous loss of physical energy and a binding of the bulk of the aggressive energies; the process lays the foundations for the inhibiting element in character.

The fighting down of sexual impulses requires much energy, attention, and "self-control." To the extent to which the biological energies of the child can no longer flow toward the outer world and into instinctual gratification, it loses its motor strength, its mobility, its courage, and its sense of reality. It becomes "inhibited." In the center of this inhibition is always the inhibition of motor activity, of running, jumping, romping, in brief, of muscular activity. One can easily observe in all patriarchal circles how children at the age of about 4, 5, or 6, become rigid, quiet, cold, and begin to armor themselves against the outer world. In this process they lose their natural charm and often become awkward, unintelligent, and "difficult to manage"; this in turn provokes an accentuation of the patriarchal methods of upbringing.

    — Wilhelm Reich, *The Sexual Revolution,*
    (trans. Theodore P. Wolfe), New York, 1969, pp. 236-237

As development in the first three stages moves toward genital dominance as opposed to rudimentary sexual drives, so the subsequent latency stage moves toward establishing the dominance of society, as opposed to the gratification of individual needs. The forces used to repress drives, to some extent necessary for ego development and sublimation of the instincts, can now form a character of such rigidity that social behavior is in jeopardy. The damage to social attitudes generally appears in neurotic symptoms at the beginning of adolescence.

Even a fairly smooth development in infancy and early childhood by no means guarantees a character able to deal with reality. The appearance of environmental obstacles utterly incompatible with a reasonable structure can retard a previously normal process of character growth. The most obvious examples are the "cases" of children who regress when put into an authoritarian educational system. These "cases" are, in fact, the norm for the underprivileged mass. Our society's institutions set immovable barriers before any attempt at non-repressive raising of the young. They relegate a psychoanalytic approach to child raising to the realm of utopian hallucinations.

Provisional Program for a Day Care Center (Charlottenburg 1)

After this brief and necessarily superficial explanation, we would like to present the provisional program of the Char-lottenburg Day Care Center. On the model of Vera Schmidt's Moscow Child Care Laboratory, the decision was made to group the children by age and, if possible, to put six to eight children in a group. At this point, there were fourteen children, all of whom, except the two in Commune 2, lived in a nuclear family as only children or as one of two siblings. We divided them into two groups, the "big kids," eight children over the age of three, and the "little kids," six two- to three-year-olds.

Though this provisional program was almost entirely a product of the concrete experiences and problems of this particular group of parents and children, it can still serve, in many ways, as a representative example. Therefore, we will summarize its various parts.

In the preface to the 15-page program written for this center we once more stated the main purpose of any nonrepressive program for young children:

The children will experience life largely through the Center. The advantage gained here is that they can more easily satisfy their basic needs in a child-collective than in an adult-dependent situation. The psychic burdens ensuing from adults' refusal of demands can be lessened where needs and interests are oriented towards other children. But this result does not follow automatically from putting the children together in a group. First of all, we must take into account the fact that parents will undertake most of the supervision in the Center; therefore, the potential of the Center, clear enough on paper, will, especially in the beginning, depend on the attitudes and conduct of the parents. This is the reason that the early stages are so important.

At that point we could define only abstractly the relationship to be developed among the three main worlds of the children: family, children's collective, and social reality (meaning the street, outsider's children, and outsiders). The ideal was "continuity of experience" between center and home. What the center permits the family must not forbid, and vice versa.

This rule was intended particularly for "sexual needs and their derivatives (cleanliness, sex play, eating, noise, mobility)." The focus was on the basic attitude towards the children's needs, not specific limitations on their activities, which would naturally differ; noisy games were not to be outlawed at home by parental needs for peace and quiet, but they could be forbidden if the apartment building prohibited noise or if the parents had to work. As for the relationship between the children's collective and the social surroundings, our guideline was "productive and active use of the contradiction between the norms of the center and those of the environment."

We must presuppose the positive nature of the children's initial stance towards their surroundings. They are fascinated with other people and children: "Why is he doing that?" "What's that?" etc. Sexual interests, although not in the abbreviated version adults know, often underlie this curiosity. The rudimentary sex drives of infancy can comprehend, eroticize, in fact transform the whole world and draw endless satisfaction from it. The proof of this . . . is the extraordinary energy of children. . . .
In the center, this is exactly the kind of freedom we want to give our children. But we will also be bringing them into conflict with the social environment, which goes by other rules; there, their outer-directed activity will be incessantly interrupted by prohibitions, limitations, and refusals. There is a danger that the children will begin to distinguish two worlds: one where "anything goes" and a larger one which forbids almost everything. . . . The worst consequence of such a division would be the children's wish to choose the center as a refuge, for in that case the contradiction between the center and its surroundings would be used, not productively and actively, but passively and with a kind of resignation. If we claim that only within the framework of the Left Wing Movement can our activity be possible and meaningful, we must then, in actual practice, create the conditions needed to let our children develop

*towards activity and productive transformation rather than
helplessness and passivity (ibid., p. 5).*

Today, in the spirit of self-criticism, we must acknowledge
that this problem proved insoluble, that we took social reality
to be mainly the petit bourgeois existence of other Berliners
instead of the life of the masses, and that we rarely broke away
from our enclaves in the petit bourgeois world.

The further contents of the program give concrete suggestions
for the center. These fall under five headings:

1. External Order in the Center
2. Toilet Training and Cleanliness
3. Conflicts Among Children
4. Play
5. Sexuality

External Order in the Center

To begin with, let us try once more to dispose of that re-
current distortion which equates nonrepressive education with
chaotic permissiveness, the kind that used to be in vogue in the
U.S.A. The center is not meant to offer children chaotic freedom;
in fact, a fixed external order is present to foster a rational mode
of action which will permit the child to put the available resources to the optimum use in gratifying his needs. Optimum
means, among other things, fulfillment while living in a collective, the chance to learn how satisfaction of any personal need
depends on the other children and their needs. . . . Chaotic
freedom causes a total absence of purposeful action; aggression,
since specific targets are missing, is nondirected. . . . Such
children grow up in a world which they will never find again in
society and are being invited, furthermore, to regress to an
emotional fixation on their parents, which is exactly what we
want to loosen up. . . .

To make our plans for the center come true, the children must
be as active as possible in planning and implementing an orderly
framework for life within it. The outer framework we planned
consisted of a well-defined daily schedule, including a collective
meal in the center, a nap and a clean-up time. We assume first
that children will be brought to the center and taken home
again at set times. This is mainly a requirement for the parents;
although there may well be exceptions made to suit the children's
wishes (refusal to stay, fears, imperative desire to do something

else); absolutely no exceptions dictated by parental wishes must occur.

Food will be cooked and served at the center. . . . This, too, should always be done at the scheduled time. . . . No child will be made to eat or to help get the meal. But if they want, the children should be able to help, whether by setting the table, for instance, or by helping with the cooking. . . . Active participation here is desirable, particularly because this is a constructive activity providing immediate need gratification.

Cleaning up the center in accordance with an adult notion of order must not interfere with such order as the children may have established, even though we usually equate their order with mess. Even though we may think that toys left lying around disturb children playing other games, we must still try to support the children's own concept of order.

Afternoon nap: the little kids will need one; should be possible for the big ones. . . . But in this case, too, we shall try to involve the children in solving this potential problem — certain children being noisy and keeping others awake.

Toilet Training and Cleanliness

We assume that the big kids will already be fully toilet trained but not the little ones. . . . We shall try, however, in the case of anality and its derivatives, to show one consistent attitude, which can be summed up as not overemphasizing cleanliness. It is important that we match our behavior to the children's, and, if interests are clearly expressed, that we follow them through — for instance, if a child is particularly interested in feces and perhaps wants to give them away as a present, we should not terminate his interest by simply quietly disposing of the excrement. This would be appropriate only if the child does not demonstrate a marked interest in his product.

In this situation we must be watchful of the process of peer group education and interfere when a child who has already learned to feel disgust expresses it ("yuk — ugh — it stinks, etc."). We should prevent children from passing on norms which contradict our principle that interest in the anal function should be satisfied and fully expressed. For the same reason (the sensory experience of other children's behavior) we must allow for some periods of regression. These need not be viewed negatively, as mere backsliding; under our guidance they can be therapeutic periods. Regression always occurs if an earlier developmental stage has been forcibly ended; because the child has not fully worked through the stage, he is left with a fixation on it. The positive value of regression is clear if we understand that a child's development (in respect to character) is never so definitive that regression can't be utilized as an opportunity to make up for interrupted interests, needs, and potentials and to carry them through to a more satisfactory outcome. Should such situations (in general, regressions, special difficulties in the anal or even genital stages, etc.) arise, we must discuss them. Hence, we will need to keep a file on each child and to study psychoanalytic theory, in order to better guide our own responses and decide when we can rely on our own therapeutic capacities and when we should consult a specialist.

One must not insist on washing hands, brushing teeth, and cleaning up in general. It is important that the children have facilities available for doing these things and can thus connect these activities with the satisfaction of anal and genital needs. The giant bathtub would be a perfect example of linking "taking a bath" with the gratification of anal and genital needs, because children not only bathe but romp around in the tub, play sex games, etc. . . .

Conflicts Among Children

The children are playing: the game is throwing blocks at some object. Suddenly, one child drops out of the game and begins throwing blocks at another child instead. Depending on the situation, we will act to try to resolve the conflict. But using what criteria? How do we act? What do we say? What are our preconceptions?

A child's conflicts and aggressions are not intrinsically bad; problems to be prevented. They are a necessary means and a necessary phenomenon in the child's encounter with reality. Children who are apparently untroubled by conflicts and aggression have usually, because of fear, just turned their aggression inward and serious inhibitions in their behavior may follow. The way we raise children, therefore, must be geared to minimizing the fear involved in socialization. To be specific, this means that we must let the children express their aggression. This creates a new problem: one child's freedom to vent his aggression shouldn't mean perpetual harassment for another.

Our discussions and experiences led us to conclude that

aggression against other children or the teacher meant that they were being used as substitutes for the parents, since the ambivalent relationship with them stops the child from openly directing his aggression towards them. This ambivalence towards the parents is caused by the Oedipal triangle, in which the parent of the same sex is seen as a rival enjoying the desired sexual relationship with the parent of the opposite sex. Expression of the hostility toward the parent of the same sex is inhibited because the child wants that parent's love and also wants to avoid punishment for his negative wishes.

The aggressions which continually arise in that area are released on other children or the teacher, the substitutes for the real target. Parents must, therefore, give their child enough psychological security to allow him, without fear, to express his hostile feelings as they occur. This means, in practice, that one must not retreat from the angry child, but instead let things take their course, even if it means being vigorously hit sometimes. Often the hostility masks tender impulses, and these, too, must be treated seriously. (Not, of course, by speedily embracing a furious child or hitting him back in a rage.)

In the center, however, aggression will be directed mainly at other children or the teacher. It is clear, from what we have already said, that we must go to the source of this aggression and change the basic conditions that produce it. Although we must intervene when another child is subjected to constant harassment or risks being physically harmed, we must first give an explanation for our behavior. If such situations arise frequently (one child hits all the others or always the same child, etc.) we must meet and discuss it to find the cause and make change possible.

Should aggression frequently be directed at the teacher — that is, the neutral person — we agreed on a ritualized way of discharging it. Since the teacher is only a parent-substitute, directing aggression at her gives no true release — denying or shrinking from this aggression would be wrong, for it would only reinforce and intensify the child's pent-up rage, causing further attacks on other children as well as mounting anxiety. If we let the child direct his anger against the teacher without incurring punishment or loss of affection, perhaps he can then grasp the objective motive for his hostility and we can encourage him to direct his aggression at its true target, his parents.

Play and Play Conditions

It seemed very important to decide whether children should be left to their own devices in play or given stimuli, some kind of framework. We thought, first of all, that the children should have the best we could give them in the way of suitable play materials. There must not only be plenty of toys but also flexible play materials at the children's disposal — things, that is, which are not ready made and can be shaped by the children themselves.

Since children's play functions to transform their experience of reality so that it can be mastered, we must give them not only things designed to be "toys," but also objects from the adult world, familiar but usually forbidden (technical equipment, radios, typewriters, etc.) or designed solely for the convenience of adults. From this principle we derive the idea that the center should not be purely a child's world, opposed to the reality the children know elsewhere. Their everyday reality is the adult world, particularly the world of their own parents. So we thought of supplying not only flexible play materials but also common household items which could be had cheaply in a junk store. However, it was important that such finds be in working order. In our discussions, we realized from our combined experiences that there comes a critical point in children's play with adults' objects at which they choose between using things for their customary purpose and changing their function. We thought simply choosing the latter meant more than the exact ways in which a child altered an object's function afterwards. The view that children repeat in play what they perceive in reality was confirmed for us, as well as the idea that the difference between a perception and its repetition lies in the shift from passive acceptance to active mastery. In the process of changing an object's function, the child manipulates his surroundings and is liberated from the fear of reality. It is very important, for this reason, to avoid interrupting the natural course of play.

On the issue of guiding this play, we arrived at the view that, in general, it is best to let the children do what they like with the play material. Like Freud, we saw play as a child's attempt to master an overwhelming adult reality and "release the tension generated by his impressions, and so to make himself, as it were, master of reality." Extended freedom and spontaneity seemed essential for releasing this tension. (We should probably make an exception of cases where adults supply a child with stimuli in order to show him new and wider possibilities.)

An important problem, even in free play, was inhibition, which we noticed sooner or later with almost every child. Especially in view of Freud's interpretation of play as the transformation of passive experience into active mastery, tempering the demand for the renunciation of instinctual gratification, freedom in play must not be cut off; when the child shows inhibitions in play, one should try to trace them to their source in order to clear them away. Severely restricted play increases the danger that a child will become neurotic due to unresolved conflicts seething within him. A child who seldom plays may retreat altogether into daydreams and work out his difficulties in that world; it is doubtful whether this play-substitute, which has no actively and productively manipulative attributes, suffices to "let him master his impressions of reality." The prerequisite for the healthy development of a child's play is, of course, that adults let him play in complete liberty. The child must not be hampered by adult morality in acting out the dictates of his unconscious mind. (Interventions to protect the child from physical harm are, of course, necessary.)

Children's Sexuality

Our unsystematic discussions, oriented to problems that just happened to come up in the conversation, didn't produce many concrete proposals for action. Basic to our thought was Wilhelm Reich's emphasis on the need to go beyond *mere tolerance* and *affirm* infantile sexuality.

The child, first of all, sees mere tolerance as a kind of non-punishment of something basically forbidden; furthermore, mere tolerance or "permitting" of sex play by no means balances the enormous pressure coming from the larger society. Explicit and unmistakable acceptance of the child's sexual life by the person who is raising him, on the other hand, can provide the basis for sex-affirming portions of the ego structure, even though one adult cannot lessen the force of negative social pressure.
        — Wilhelm Reich, *The Collapse of Sexual Morality*,
   Copenhagen, 1935, p. 6

We conclude: the acceptance of infantile sexuality must be obvious in every attitude and word of an adult. And this is precisely the point at which continuity between center and home is vital. While trying to raise these children in our own way, it will be important to recognize that many, especially the older ones, will have already learned to repress their sexual needs, or at least to accept society's moral standards. If the children have already built up disgust and repugnance concerning genital or infantile sexuality, we may find it hard to achieve our educational goals.

The biggest obstacle we encountered while trying to instill an affirmative attitude to sex in our children was the parents' own repressed sexuality. Mere intellectual recognition of the importance of infantile sexuality does not eliminate guilt about sex, well rooted in the unconscious.

There will be negative effects if, while the adults verbally accept and affirm the child's sex play, his sexual pleasure and satisfaction, they simultaneously show disgust, fear or skepticism in nonverbal ways. For instance, if children stick things into vagina or anus or poke around with their fingers, etc., parents often, because of their own problems, will be disgusted or want to avoid the sight, feelings which they rationalize as concern for the children's safety. Of course, such concern may well be justified, in which case, one might gently advise the child to be careful not to hurt his genitals. If children are careful, they can also play with each other's genitals; working out the awareness of sexual difference (penis envy) can thus be eased.

Once a child has established sexual repressions, he may express those needs only in a sublimated way. We must try to help him express them more openly. Some children, for example, conceal their intense interest in sexual problems, dropping the topic as quickly as they have brought it up, or they may be too timid to ask questions. In such cases we have to pursue the matter with our children, explain it to them, and try to reawaken their interest. If the children want information, we will not overwhelm them with encyclopedic explanations but orient our answers to the interests which they have voiced. In giving explanations, of course, we must be as truthful as possible; and general agreement on the use of unambiguous language would make sense.

We also discussed whether and in what way children should find out about the sexual activity of their parents. In discussing whether children should watch their parents have intercourse, we couldn't reach a definitive conclusion. We should discuss this question again. We did agree, at any rate, on the importance of considering whether the child would, in this situation, feel completely left out. Parents should avoid creating an atmosphere of total exclusion, so the answer to this question probably depends on their ability to control their love-making so as not to wholly exclude the child.

Perhaps we should reemphasize that our purpose was not to instigate sexual expression or play in our children, but only to pay careful attention to their sexual strivings, to prevent potential inhibitions by trying to ensure that there was a shared satisfaction in play of those needs that are, in the broadest sense, sexual. Obviously the children were allowed, if they felt like it, to go around the center naked, to go to the toilet in pairs or groups, and to masturbate. Different individuals at different times made extensive use of these rights, usually showing some erotic imagination, as, for example, when they painted each other's bodies with water colors.

For two reasons we will not describe in detail children's sexuality as expressed in such a group and influenced by a favorable environment. First, we are still analyzing our material (there are hundreds of notebooks covering the Charlottenburg center alone) and comparing our findings with data from other centers as well as traditional child rearing organizations. We do not think it makes scientific sense to generalize prematurely. A few significant examples, like those just given, are all we need to present now.

The second reason for our reticence concerns our past experience in issuing·reports on the centers. West German colleagues frequently understood specific practices to be binding rules, which would be applied without modification in a completely different context, naturally producing disastrous results.

This is no more "merely mistaken" an interpretation than the superficial and entirely incoherent press coverage of the Day Care Centers (cf. chapter 3). One can find hundreds of examples to illustrate nonrepressive methods of education, but unless they are taken in their social and political context they will all remain mystifying. What we "do" about masturbation in a three-year-old is determined not only by our knowledge of biological and psychological facts pertaining to childhood sexuality but also by our grasp of the way in which the repression of sexuality helps maintain the authoritarian nuclear family and the capitalistic system. In the final analysis, the specific techniques of repression are a product of class situation and class consciousness, or the lack of it.*

Although bourgeois-liberal teachers may understand the sociological factors which bear on child raising, their dilemma is not altered. They see teaching as an individualistic profession and therefore limit their suggestions to (a) isolated "educational reforms," and (b) vague appeals to "humanity." They do not touch upon the fact that to revolutionize the present system of raising children, fundamental political change is a necessity.

Part of the mystification emanating from bourgeois educational theory results from proposals and programs which can have no possible effect on the fate of the children in question. We shall support this statement in a more appropriate place. This is another reason for our wish to avoid making, in this book, specific recommendations for conduct suitable for nonrepressive educators. Detached from the socialist movement and the struggle for basic social change, such ideas, if accepted, would work eventually against our political goals.

Therefore, we shall present only a few examples of the centers' methods in order to let the reader visualize the situation.

Remarks on the "Sexual Revolution"

We do want to discuss briefly two closely related misunderstandings. First, people often think that the sexual revolution of recent years, despite its many drawbacks, at least managed to liberate sex in Germany from bourgeois taboos. It is true, of course, that the idea peddlers, the producers of magazines, books, and movies, have used the topic more and more enthusiastically. Sexual practices may actually have changed: extra- and premarital sex and the Pill have surely become more widespread (at least in middle class circles), and one cannot ignore the growing incidence of divorce, organized exchanges of partners, and group sex. But just how small a "revolution" this has been in the everyday lives of the general population is revealed by a recent questionnaire survey of the 23-year-olds in Hamburg — a sizeable metropolis. Only 7 percent of the women and 24 percent of the men approve of sexual intercourse with no plans for marriage. In the conscious-

---

*Advice on education that does not put the primary emphasis on political issues remains an idealistic pursuit, just enlightening enough to help critical members of the privileged class and to enhance their own power.

ness of 23-year-olds, moreover, sexual compatibility has almost nothing to do with preserving a marriage. Asked what they thought *would* be important here, only 2 percent of the women and 3 percent of the men checked "sexual compatibility," but 67 percent and 88 percent respectively checked "love, trust, understanding, frank discussions"

— Pfeil and others, *The Twenty-Three-Year-Olds: An Inquiry into the Generation Born in 1941*, Tubingen, 1968

Closer examination shows that the "sexual revolution" (as proclaimed by the mass media) is just a new version of the same old double standard.

The patriarchal family has never been able to satisfy sexual needs. The entire history of the family shows it to require assistance from prostitution and from sexual exploitation of economic dependents. With the increasing tendency to apply capitalist commodity thinking to human relations and the disappearance of patriarchal authority, sex has finally come to be treated as a commodity within the family structure; organized exchanges of partners occur (Commune 2, op. cit., p. 7).

It is easy enough to show that the trend to "free trade" in sexual practices, though it does carry the ideological premises of the nuclear family to the point of absurdity, does not really endanger the institution. Just one of the suggestions from the "new sex priests," such as Kölle, will suffice: they recommend an occasional extramarital adventure just so that the lifelong sexual partners can recapture their pleasure in each other. As long as the nuclear family survives — ultimately, for economic reasons — sexual freedom serves as a sad little palliative for daily surfeit and disgust. In other words, even if people played around ten times more than ever before, it would not add up to real sexual liberation. For merely to amass orgasms, even if man and woman arrive at them simultaneously, is not really to satisfy sexual needs. In *Sexuality and the Class Struggle*, Reimut Reiche gives this point detailed attention. He stresses the fact that a fully developed genital sexuality presupposes, not the denial of partial drives (oral and anal needs, tenderness, warmth, etc.) (cf. *Early Infantile Sexuality*), but only their subordination.

Even to speak of "subordination" is to put far too much emphasis on the role of repression in the integration of partial drives during sexual maturation. One cannot imagine, surely, that repressive forces control the integration of partial drives to form a fully developed genital character capable of pleasure. A "genital character," which corresponds with the development of genital sexuality, is capable of controlling as well as affirming the instincts, capable of achievement, work, and discipline as well as self-surrender and spontaneity. The actual development of these two sides of the psyche, the relative strength of one or the other of these tendencies, is part of the individual personality and depends on the degree of his subordination of all drives to the reality principle (adaptation), his flight from reality or his involuntary obedience to it (virtue as bowing to the reality principle). Characters who fulfill the genital norms of a culture — specifically our society — in a forced and rigid way, cannot be termed genital characters without some qualification. Their social and sexual behavior can indicate that they have not developed a true genital character structure, but are too weak to meet the social norms and too weak to rebel against them; hence they must suppress any expression of their unintegrated partial drives and they arrive at a pseudo-genital, rigid behavior. Such behavior I shall call the "genital façade" (op. cit., pp. 74ff.).

As Reich argues, with ample empirical support, "sexual liberation" must be seen, above all, as the prerogative of the privileged classes.

This is equally true of child raising. In the last few years, we have been deluged with reports and enlightened articles (in magazines such as our *Eltern* and *Es*). They all feed on the fear of childhood neurosis, damage to intelligence, and, in general, on the recent "fear of our children" (title of the best seller by Zulliger). But uncomfortable feelings, of course, don't mean serious questioning of the nuclear family. For the same reason, suppression of children's drives will not diminish markedly. The "liberation" of infantile sexuality really turns out to be subtle repression rather than open prohibition or threats like those Freud repeatedly reports. We just say it differently today:

If you discover your small child in some sort of sex play alone or with others, you'll probably be at least a little bit surprised and shocked. In expressing your disapproval it's better to be firmly matter-of-fact rather than very shocked or angry. You want him to know that you don't want him to do it, but you don't want him to feel that he's a criminal. You can say, for instance, "Mother

*doesn't want you to do that again," or "That isn't polite," and
shoo the children to some other activity.*
                        — Benjamin Spock, *Baby and Child Care,*
                        Pocket Books, New York, 1971 edition, p. 373

Spock and others, years after their countryman, Kinsey, established empirically the fact that children masturbate in a completely
sexual way and reach normal orgasms (cf. description of masturbation of a three-year-old girl in *Sexual Behavior of the Human
Female,* p. 106), are still trying to explain away infantile sexuality.
Kurt Seelmann, Consultant on Child Raising, psychotherapist,
and head of the Munich Youth Program, makes the same sort of
suggestions in his book (100,000 copies sold) for German parents.

*If the child holds his penis occasionally, we needn't say a word
about it. But if he does this frequently, then we should, in a friendly way, ask the reason. We should not, under any circumstances,
just forbid the child's behavior, punish him, or simply say, "That
isn't done." His clothes may itch or be too tight; a rough pair of
underpants may be tickling or bothering him. We have already
pointed out that since the skin of this area is especially densely
covered with nerve endings, it is especially liable to irritation. It's
a specially bad place for clothes to be too tight. Some children
should not wear wool next to the skin in this area. But if it turns
out that the playing around and touching is due to desire, specifically, a desire to explore and enjoy the sensitivity of the region,
then we have been leaving our child alone too much and giving
him too few stimulating occupations. He needs toys. He should
have stimulating playmates. To divert him from this habit, he
should be rewarded over and over again when he shows signs of
pleasure in play and work. In this as in other things, abrupt
methods will not be effective. Such methods only make the child
hide what he is doing and we then lose our control over him.*
    — Kurt Seelmann, *How Shall I Tell My Child the Facts of Life?,*
    3rd. ed., Munich. 1967

Not quite as Machiavellian as Seelmann, but implicitly no less
absolutist, is the *Sex Information Handbook* put out by the Federal
Office for Health and intended as a guide for sex education in the
schools and similar institutions. It is absolutely silent on the subject of infantile sexuality. Three sentences, of a purely ornamental
nature, dispose of childhood development:

64   Chapter 2

*The second stage of development is characterized by a fairly
steady rate of maturation. It consists of the period from the third
year to the attainment of sexual maturity. The replacement of
teeth occurs during this period. Toward the end of this period,
largely due to the change in the jawline, childish features disappear and the total character of the child appears ready for the
decisive developments of puberty.*

     — *Sexual Information Handbook: Biological Information
      on the Sexuality of Man,* 1969

    The *Sex Information Handbook* — exemplifying the "progres-
sive trend in education," according to the reactionary Family
League and other lobbies now fighting its subversive influence —
has a simple solution to the problem of infantile sexuality: deny
its existence!

**Implementing the Program: Physical Arrangement and Daily
Schedule in Charlottenburg I**

Introduction
    Our rooms in Jebenstrasse 1, a monumental office building of
Nazi vintage, were at the top on the fifth and sixth floors. In contrast to the storefronts, this space was amply supplied with light,
heat, and rugs, and was, as well, near the zoo and the park. We
hardly disturbed the other tenants, since we were the only occu-
pants on our floors. One disadvantage of these quarters was their
total isolation from any social surroundings, such as neighbors,
streets, and neighborhood life in general; we tried to compensate
for this by going on outings and walks. The rooms opened onto a
huge roof terrace which we had planned to use as a playground,
but building code restrictions forbade it. Anyway, we couldn't
have afforded to arrange it as a playground. That was also the
reason we never set up the giant plastic bathtub.
    Because we had a sculptor and an architect in the parent group,
our ideas about furnishings were, at first, mainly oriented to contemporary design and materials, but eventually our plans came
down to a few elements of plastic and steel. Traditional education
still expects children to learn about their environment through
anachronistic materials from a remote era of civilization. We
assumed that neither a place which reverted to some vignette of

Victorian domesticity nor one totally dominated by functionalism
(postwar architecture) could produce a positive mastery of the
environment. After many discussions, we chose an arrangement
intended to meet both the smaller children's need for warmth and
coziness and the older ones' need to make contact with the technologically advanced environment. We tried to consider the children's own wishes in every decision we made and also to involve
them in the practical work.

In the large room (18 ft. by 33 ft.) assigned to the older children
we set up shelves to hold play and craft materials, a Formica table,
and several little chairs which could be adjusted to two different
heights and used to build, for instance, trains or towers. We covered a low platform with mattresses and big foam pillows encased
in plastic; these large and soft materials served as mats for jumping and romping about. A big blackboard covered one wall. Swings
and a rope hung in the middle of the room. We also had a guinea
pig in a box. Certain play materials, though we were always ex-
changing them for others or altering them to suit our needs,
proved useful:

Large objects like cardboard refrigerator boxes, useable as
houses, caves, etc.; wooden barrels with holes drilled in them,
ladders, bouncing balls.

Craft materials: all kinds of paints and brushes, rolls of paper
(donated by some newspaper printers), clay, plaster, construction
paper, etc. — whatever the children wished and the parents and
teachers dreamed up: For the older children, besides all the above,
nails and boards, etc.

For play and learning: dolls, bears, railroads, toy cars, blocks,
picture books, card games, etc. In addition, things from the adult
world such as typewriters, radios, complicated kitchen equipment,
which the children could handle and thus remove from the "un-
touchable" category. Everything was either put on the shelves or
distributed about the room in such a way that the children could
use anything at any time. Magazines and posters, to cut up and
use for collages, were also popular.

The smaller rooms for the younger children had a similar physical arrangement: table, shelves, chairs, blackboard. We also
brought in a wooden podium, which stood about shoulder height,
with side openings about two feet high. We put mattresses inside,
intending it to serve as a sleeping place for the little ones and as a
cave for doll play, sex play, etc. We opened the partition between
the rooms in several places so that the children could crawl

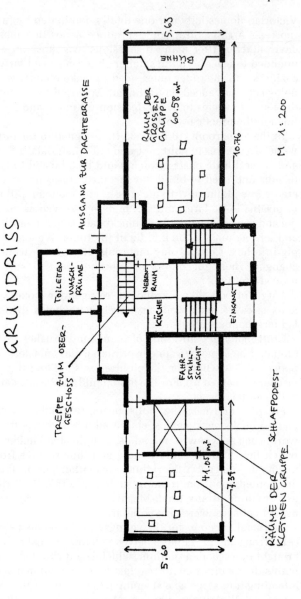

RÄUME DES KINDERLADENS CHARLOTTENBURG I
JEBENSTRASSE 1, 5. ETAGE
GRUNDRISS

M 1:200

BÜHNE

RAUM DER GROSSEN GRUPPE
60.58 m²

AUSGANG ZUR DACHTERRASSE

5.63

10.76

TOILETTEN & WASCH-RÄUME

NEBEN-RAUM

KÜCHE

EINGANG

TREPPE ZUM OBER-GESCHOSS

FAHR-STUHL-SCHACHT

SCHLAFPODEST

RÄUME DER KLEINEN GRUPPE

41.05 m²

7.34

5.60

through, hide and peer through the window-like openings.

The building had toilets and washrooms, but unfortunately no shower or bath. We put wooden stools under the sinks so that the children could manage by themselves. We installed a kitchen in the lobby between the two rooms which could provide hot or cold meals for 10 to 15 children. There was also a counter where the children could get drinks or food for themselves or a friend. In the lobby we put hooks within the children's reach for them to hang up their clothes, and we set up orange crate shelves in the next room for underwear, mittens, etc.

After the group of smaller children moved out in the fall of 1969, we used the upper floor, originally planned as a dining room, as a craft and work room. At that time, too, the nearby music conservatory offered us an empty lot. We put in an old car, sand, and tires and used it for a playground.

Fixing up the rooms took about two months. This was also the time of the outings we mentioned earlier and the theoretical discussions, which were held once or twice a week. Division of labor was based on the collective's rule of barter, according to which those who could spend less time earning a living (those who lived in the collective, held scholarships, got parental support, or had private savings) did more of the work than those who had more economic obligations (students on a work-study program, workers, professionals). Though everyone agreed, in principle, with this way of handling things, problems often came up because, obviously, everybody was not equally interested in manual work. The misunderstandings required discussions to resolve them. We found that we could only partially adhere to our original principle; that in order to keep work free of alienating effects and coercive pressure to achieve, people should work only when they wanted. The reason was that, though all had the same practical concern — to get the center set up — many individuals, after years of study and research, had lost interest in manual work. This meant that those whose professions (sculptor, architect, housewife) involved such work also "wanted" to do most of it. Only gradually did we become aware of these problems; then we instituted "work nights" when the division of labor was suspended, everyone worked together, and some comrades shared their knowledge of particular materials with the others.

Daily Schedule
The day at the center began at 10 a.m. Since not all parents

could get into the habit of bringing the children on time, thus causing the teacher much trouble, threats of punishment were necessary to produce a full recognition of the need for some degree of order. Most of the children came by car and that job was given to the parents with cars.

Besides the full time teacher, one parent came every day to help with shopping, cooking, and cleaning up. Members of student workshops, who were supposed to be observing the class for a course, sometimes came. Students in the film school began an 8 mm. film, but they were forced to interrupt the project when they were expelled from school for political disruptions. We always tried to keep the number of adults to a minimum, for they tended to distract the children too much.

A meal was served about 1 o'clock. As much as possible, we involved the children in preparing it. Shopping was often combined with a walk, which also served to teach the children how to behave in traffic and sometimes led to finding things for afternoon play (boxes, stones, chestnuts, sticks, ice cream cups, etc.).

The afternoon was usually spent in more or less organized play, interrupted periodically by children drinking cocoa and eating some cake or fruit. Some children took a nap. We never tried to make them all sleep at the same time; or if we did, we soon abandoned the idea. As soon as the children got used to the new environment, they learned to meet their own needs and to lie down when they were tired, although it's true that the little children needed some guidance. In the fall of 1969 the smaller group left the center, because their needs were different and did not combine harmoniously with those of the bigger group. Then too, there were problems when some of the bigger children could not handle their aggression within their own group and took it out on the smaller children. In the new center in the Pohlstrasse the little children stayed overnight once a week and had no problems about going to sleep. Around 5 o'clock they were taken home, usually in groups. Some children made plans to go to a friend's and spend the night. We always encouraged this, unless a child consistently wished to sleep away from home, and then we tried to find the reason.

Occasionally, to free ourselves for important meetings or demonstrations, we organized parental supervision for the weekends. But usually we took the children along to political events, because their participation as a children's collective helped their group process and gave them a confrontation with reality. We organized parties on birthdays, as well as parties just for the fun of it. Children also wanted to be together during the weekends and visited each other's homes. We arranged Sunday clean-up shifts to rotate among parents.

Should Parents Take Turns Working or Hire an "Outsider"?

While the parents of the Charlottenburg group believed all along that only an outsider (a kindergarten teacher, male or female) could reduce the children's fixation on their parents and support the growth of a children's collective, the Schöneberg center adhered for a long time to the principle of using only parents. They explained their views in INFO 6 (Berlin, March 1969):

Advantages of Rotating the Work of Supervision Among Parents
1. Political Considerations:

a) The parents are developing a sense of solidarity within the adult group and with the children.

b) Self-education and self-discipline emerge in response to political demands.

c) The strivings of all participants towards liberation are fostered in the socialist day care center by cooperative practical and political work — in this case, by undertaking the work of supervision on a rotating basis.

d) Responsibility is not delegated to an "authority" (the teacher). This protects against privatization and escape from the political struggle.

e) The parents' intensive work in their child's world outside the home fulfills a major tenet of socialist child rearing: no separation of adult and juvenile worlds. That separation has a class character and is destructive. The work of supervision helps create a comradeship in struggle based not on authority structures but on solidarity. Practical educational and political work thus constitutes a part of private family life.

2. Psychological Considerations:

a) Children develop a more flexible, richer spectrum of social attitudes and relationships when, after a preliminary stabilizing period of about two years, during which one person cares for them, they are confronted with a variety of individuals and cease to be fixated on one (cf. R. Spitz).

b) Children get a variety of possibilities for identification and experience of different personalities, giving them a broader basis for intellectual development.

c) Children have the opportunity to make conscious choices, to learn preferences for different kinds of adult behavior, and to judge what they dislike, in accordance with their needs. No single type of behavior is held up as the universal rule. The children's criticisms, in turn, teach the adults something.

d) Continuity between home and center can be maintained. There was no disparity to make the children insecure, to aggravate their problems and neutralize the advantages of educational experiences outside the home.

e) Since an emotional fixation on one authority figure cannot exist, the children's collective speeds the process of socialization and encourages autonomous behavior and initiative. The children see the adult more as an ally of their group than as someone who imposes order from above.

f) Through the experience of sharing parents, parents and children become less possessive towards each other and develop a wider circle of trust (cf. extended family).

Disadvantages of Rotation

1. Time and Energy Required.
2. Neurotic Personalities:

a) Six neurotic parents are worse than one neurotic teacher.

b) The participants must be psychologically able to give the children a firm ground for trust, through which the children can fully develop their capacities. The children must not be prevented, by continual experiences of estrangement, from developing a stable personality.

c) A troubled parent-child relationship produces difficulties and behavior problems in that child when his parents are taking their turn as "teacher."

While it took the Schöneberg center a long time to relinquish their belief in supervision by parents alone, our group found out very quickly that only a few parents could act in a way that did not breed neurotic behavior in the children. Children who were strongly attached to their parents waged, on the days when their parents were working in the center, an unending war of jealousy; they could not develop relationships with anyone else's parents, who were, in turn, jealously claimed by their own children. Since we all had had little experience with children, we tended to leave the children on their own too much and to give them too little constructive stimulation. In conflict situations, on the other hand, to stop violence we tended to intervene too soon. The teacher was more consistent than the parents in her pattern of intervention and in enforcing other types of restraint, as well as in her methods of stimulating the children.

The problem, generally, was not to provide "possibilities for varied identifications" with adults, as the Schöneberg paper says, but to get the children out of their authoritarian family structure and develop their ability to pursue their interests in the framework of a children's collective. But the parents' unconscious fixation on their children outweighed their good intentions and blocked this process.

We could see that conflicts rooted in the parent-child relationship were, if not eliminated, at least alleviated by prolonged exposure to the teacher. At regular intervals, we compared the teacher's reports with the image of the parents revealed in transcripts and self-descriptions to try to understand the problems which kept cropping up with some children. We must admit, however, that our rather voluntaristic approach and our layman's version of psychoanalysis rarely led to improvements demonstrably connected to our therapeutic techniques. We considered setting up a psychoanalytic center where trained therapists could supervise parents and children in the collective, but we couldn't find any psychoanalysts eager to work politically with left wing groups. Without the objective perspective of the teacher, however, we could neither have eliminated the rationalizations which individual parents used to obscure their relationships with their children, nor could we have arrived at any true understanding of the children's behavior.

The possibility that parents would gradually delegate all responsibility to the "authority" of the teacher (as noted above) proved to be a real danger in all the groups at one time or another. The risk, however, cannot be avoided simply by having the parents do more practical work in the center, but only by trying to detach the political viewpoint of each individual from its individualistic roots, creating through regular discussions the type of political consciousness which would allow each person to devote all his energy to building a real socialist movement.

It was expecting too much of the children's collectives to demand that they function as fully realized models of socialist practice. For the teacher herself, the new professional experience in the center was a means to personal and political emancipation, because her potential as an educator and a human being was not crippled by an authoritarian system, crowded classrooms, or a rigid daily schedule.

Experience Leads to New Insights

The further history of the Charlottenburg center shows three major areas in which the program might have been improved:

1. Systematic group learning of specific social skills (from tying shoelaces to answering the phone or finding one's way around the city, depending on the developmental stage and interests shown by the children). This means the participants could be more concerned with creating a positive preschool curriculum.

2. The principle of resolution of group conflicts by the group itself and resolution of individual problems through unrestricted play should be complemented by structured group activity. All the children should be integrated into the group, e.g., by therapeutic role playing, self-presentation in dramatic form, music, dance, etc.

3. Play and learning should be shared with other children who were not raised in nonrepressive institutions, especially children from other social classes (more on this later).

On the whole, the Charlottenburg program was meant to counteract therapeutically the personality deformations caused by the children's prior years in the nuclear family. The goal during the first period was to clear away in group play the individual fixations and inhibitions which the children brought with them. At this time, we favored individual regression in order to get a fresh working through of earlier stages of development.

As the children's collective progressed, it became clear that we had underestimated the significance of aggression. The children acted out their feelings more and more frequently. They bothered each other in play, beat each other up, threw things at each other, and sometimes groups attacked the teacher, especially when she was trying to settle a fight. Since the teacher was becoming more powerless by the day, we had to do something.

The problem of aggression provoked vigorous discussion within the center. The issue of physical aggression, like that of using force in political actions, could only be relieved of its ideological ballast by a slow process of enlightenment.

Both problems are connected to the basic dualism which dictates the role aggression plays in highly industrialized capitalist societies. Morally, aggression is frowned upon and considered an emotion to be discarded — "uncivilized behavior." In reality, it permeates, in varying degrees of visibility, all important aspects of social behavior. People admire the "man who makes it" in professional life by elbowing his way up. In leisure activities, aggression manifests itself in driving; it is obvious in sport and is passively discharged by watching movies or television; within the family aggression appears in the oppression of wife and children. The force that is continually transmitted downwards through the social hierarchy can, in the end, be discharged with impunity on social scapegoats. In fact, it makes them necessary — foreign labor, students, hippies, Negroes, yesterday the Jews and today the Arabs. While the brutal tactics used against these groups are, at most, deplored, force directed from the bottom up is considered a contemptible and criminal act. For example, while the Springer Press was free to use hate campaigns to program the assassin Bachmann to his act (*Bild* helped pull the trigger on Rudi Dutschke), even liberals become indignant about broken windows and burning cars. While the Chicago "conspirators" were condemned to long prison sentences, the policemen who killed three Negroes in those same demonstrations still go free. Public indignation, belatedly but justly aroused against the brutality of the American military machine by the disclosure of previously suppressed information about the massacre at My Lai, has been diverted by "scientific" considerations ("Were the soldiers under the influence of drugs?") to a detour which, ultimately, will direct it against ghetto blacks and hippies. One can think of innumerable other examples.

The same rules apply to child raising. Parents and teachers are absolutely free to strike children, to yell at them, and to use all sorts of psychological weapons such as the withdrawal of love or threats. No one gets upset until a child turns to crime or dies from mistreatment. But God help the child who dares to show open aggression against his parents. The ideological premise of innate aggression that must be suppressed, the theoretical prop for the whole authoritarian structure, even now receives fresh reinforcements from many scholars.

Concerning the Origins of Destructiveness

Is the assumption of inborn evil in man justified? Is it, as all reactionaries say, the reason that wars, suffering, and oppression have always existed? Wilhelm Reich thoroughly examined this question:

> Aggression, in the strict sense, has nothing to do with sadism or destruction. The word means "going towards." Every active expression of life is aggressive — sexual pleasure seeking activity as well as destructive, hate-filled acts; sadistic as well as supportive behavior. Aggression is the expression of life by the muscular system, by the system of motor action. This point has an extremely important bearing on present child raising styles. Much of the aggression which we force our children to subdue to their own detriment results from confusing "agressive" with "malicious" or "sexual." In every case, the reason for agression is the possibility that some vital need could be satisfied. Agression is not, therefore, a drive with an inherent end, but the immediate means of implementing a drive in action. This action is aggressive because the tension within the organism pushes for satisfaction. Hence there is destructive, sadistic, locomotive and coordinative, and sexual aggression.
>
> If the satisfaction of aggressive sexuality is blocked, the inner pressure still seeks an outlet. Thus appears the impulse to use any possible means to find satisfaction. Aggression begins to drown out love. If the pleasure drive is blocked entirely, made unconscious or suppressed by anxiety, aggression, originally just a means to an end, becomes in itself a way to release tension, the pleasurable expression of life. This is the origin of sadism. . . .
>
> Destruction for the sake of destruction is the organism's response to the denial of the basic satisfactions in life, especially sexual ones.
>
> — Wilhelm Reich, The Function of the Orgasm, Cologne, 1969, p. 137

From these observations one can make two generalizations about collective child raising:

1. A child's aggression must be acted out as completely as possible, even if it involves physical attacks on others. For this is the only way that we can find out, with the child, the source of the aggression and the instinctual drive underlying it. The more this acting out is blocked, the more it is deflected from its original target and the more impetus it gains as an independent impulse towards destructive behavior. But acting out must, of course, be restricted if it oppresses other children or directly

endangers them through attacks with sharp objects, etc. These limits must be clearly explained to the child and must be enforced with consistency.

2. We should not offer the children substitute objects for their aggression, as, for example, in Japan, where workers in some factories can take out their aggression on inflatable rubber models of the owner.

One teacher's journal from the early period will illustrate how these principles relate to conflicts in the center:

I often intervene with I. and M. (both just four years old), because otherwise they would really hurt each other. M. and I. throw cars at each other or stick pencils in each other's backs. It's pointless to explain to them that this is dangerous. I. and M. have terrific fights — biting and scratching. When N. has been playing with I. and P., M. will fight with N. too, throwing things at him, pinching him. All the children except Mi. are now against M. and are scared of him. They shut M. out and don't want to let him play.

M., realizing that the others shrink from him when he screams and attacks them, begins suggesting games which come to appeal to the others.

During the meal, the children get involved in spitting milk at each other and I realize that I don't know how to cope with M.'s anger, which is always flaring up again. I come nowhere near its source. I am aware that I am interfering with some process. . . . M.'s rage grows worse as time goes on. He is just holding himself back from attacking P. and Mi. I speak with M. about it and ask him why he hits the others and makes them angry so that they won't play with him any more.

The children then ask him to stop. M. says he will.

I don't know how much his behavior, which is now a little less aggressive, has been affected by my stepping in and pointing out to him that the others are backing off from him, but I think I have to intervene when he disrupts the others' play to such an extent (Notes of 4.9.68).

This example illustrates a learning process which can lead from aggressive oppression to a more social type of behavior. But the deeper causes of M.'s continual aggressive behavior are not touched upon. We can well understand that, on the whole, this big, strong boy who stayed at the center for two months, became a kind of bogie for the others. After he left we made an amazing discovery: for a time, the other children would take turns in assuming, in the manner appropriate to their particular character structure, the role of aggressive oppressor. At first we thought that this was an unalterable constellation of forces in each individual case; for instance, we noticed that many people thought N. mentally and physically stronger than the rest of the children. Finally, we realized that psychological conflicts were concealed by this behavior. Another journal entry about this:

Afternoon in the Schöneberg Center.

When we arrive, the children rush off to play with bicycles, scooters, baby carriages, and trains. Later on, blocks, cooking materials and books win some passing attention.

Gr. (three-year-old girl) screams; she wants the baby carriage that Ni. (three-year-old girl) is playing with and goes to T. (teacher). T. says: "Go on, ask her!" N., overhearing this, grabs the carriage from Ni. and wants to give it to Gr. Ni. begins to scream. T.: "Settle it yourselves." They do, after N. abandons the carriage.

A scooter that has been left lying around gets in N.'s way. He wants T. to put it away. She refuses and he screams, "Someone's got to put it away!!" He keeps screaming until Ni. and K. (three-year-old girl) do it.

N. frequently interferes in conflicts that come up in the group and rigorously upholds the "rights" of one party; he always favors G. in particular, but otherwise he plays alone. He makes the rounds of all the groups in the room twice and hits the children in them with no apparent warning or provocation, striking them on the face, back, or arms (Notes for 7.8.68).

Anyone who can enter imaginatively into this situation will see immediately that behind the role of policeman which N. assumes lies the wish to play with the others. Some experience, some conflict, prevents him from entering into normal relationships.

At the next parents' meeting, inquiry into the causes of N.'s behavior led, not too surprisingly, to the influence of tension in his parents' marriage and conflicts in the home. N.'s needs for tenderness and attention could not be adequately satisfied. We asked N.'s father, therefore, to pay special attention to N. and, above all, to respond to any desire N. might express for affection and tenderness.

N. soon found a way to act out the needs and frustrations behind his aggression: what we called the "kitten game" gave him the chance. By pretending to be a helpless and affectionate little pet, he could permit his father and the children in the center to pet him, take care of him, and nurture him — a game he would play for hours.

The children themselves understood the purpose of the "kitten game" and used it later in resolving similar conflicts.

A description from a report by Commune 2 lets us see how the inhibition of aggression, acquired from bourgeois life, can be dissolved:

Nessim, who previously didn't dare to act out any aggression against his father now openly show negative feelings towards Eike. He hits him, wants to kill him, expresses death wishes towards him, saying, "You have one more day to live." Undoubtedly, the children's group and the Commune helped to free the hostile side of his ambivalent feelings toward his father. Journal, April 1969: Eike is fixing the midday meal. Nessim keeps urging Eike to go off with him alone. Eike says, "But I can't. I have to cook for the others." In the afternoon they would normally go home by car with the other children, but Nessim wants to take the bus home with his father. "We could do that," says Eike, "but I'd rather go home with the others. It's raining and if we took the bus we'd have to walk through it." Nessim is pretty angry. He goes to I. and arranges to spend the night at his house. Outside, Eike asks him if he still wouldn't rather drive to the Commune (he realizes that Nessim only wants to spend the night somewhere else because he was angry about not getting his way). I. then says to Eike: "You don't own Nessim. He can do whatever he wants." The children leave with I.'s father.

This example shows that children in a collective can work through their aggressive feelings towards their parents. We cannot as yet define the effect of being in a children's collective and a commune on conflicts like the Oedipus complex. But we can at least hypothesize, in regard to the implications for socialization, that the collective lets children work through, on a conscious level, the negative side of their ambivalent feelings about their parents. They are not obliged to repress them, as generally happens in the nuclear family. Repressed aggressive energies, therefore, are neither turned inward nor left unresolved as feelings which later can be manipulated against society's official scapegoats. If the child can disentangle all his ambivalent impulses towards those who govern his life, he can turn his aggression against the cause of his oppression in a realistic way. Ego-strength is the result. "If this hate remains conscious, it can be a mighty revolutionary force within each individual; it can be the means to sever ties to the family and can easily be channelled to the rational aim of fighting the conditions which produced the hate."

— Wilhelm Reich, *The Sexual Revolution*, p. 122

Political Education

We have not yet covered one important point in our program for Charlottenburg I — political education.

After the centers became generally known, accusations of "indoctrination," "violating a child's trust," and "communistic hate compaigns" were frequently made. Behind these phrases lies the ideological myth of a happy childhood far away from the world, well-protected by parents. This myth requires total disregard of the fact that from the age of one a child is educated to obedience, cleanliness, and order, to train him for bourgeois social life, and to "indoctrinate" him so powerfully and so effectively that most people never notice it! We must reiterate that education in a class society cannot be neutral and value-free. As we pointed out in our introduction, it is imbued with a class character in its aims and in its methods.

This is the difference between the present type of political education and a socialist one: while the veil of objectivity — which usually goes unnoticed by teachers — in bourgeois education permits the efficient transmission of the major norms of the present society, our task is to expose the ideological nature of bourgeois education; that is, we must bring its political character to the surface in order to fight it, while simultaneously passing on a different content. The hypocrisy of indignation about political indoctrination of children is best illustrated by the shocking examples from the third world, where children, whether they like it or not, are drawn into the battle.

Vo Thie Lien, a twelve-year-old girl and a survivor of My Lai, toured Europe in 1970 to tell of the atrocities she had witnessed to raise funds for the National Liberation Front. The *Frankfurter Rundschau* and other bourgeois papers, scandalized by the spectacle, asked how one could make a child participate in this "ghastly exhibition"; whether it wouldn't cause psychological

damage; and wasn't a twelve-year-old entitled to just "be a child?"
These outraged individuals entirely forgot that this particular
child had never *been* a "child" as they understood the word, that
the atrocities which they were shocked to hear from a child's
mouth had been her daily life.

Vo Thie Lien herself parried their worries about Communists
using an innocent child for propaganda and turning her into a
"puppet" by her display of independent thought, vouched for by
Bruckner, the psychoanalyst. She asked one journalist, "Wouldn't
you fight if every year the Americans came into your town to take
away the rice crop?" The kind of political consciousness which
the Viet Cong developed by political agitation was her only hope
of understanding the events of her life and integrating them into
her thought. By actively struggling against the imperialist oppressor, she ceased to be just a helpless victim of circumstance. The
horror of total war waged by the American aggressor on the whole
population, including the children, of Vietnam and making the
whole people the political enemy shattered in this case the illusion
that childhood is an untroubled no man's land.

Quick voiced exactly the same kind of indignation in its articles
on a training camp for Al Fatah, the Palestinian Freedom Movement: "Children are being taught to kill." The parents of these
children were driven from their homeland more than twenty
years ago by the Zionists and have been waiting ever since in
miserable refugee camps for the "peaceful solution" that never
came. Their dreams of a life worthy of human beings were shattered a thousand times. They saw that the promises of imperialists
and reactionaries were nothing but lies. The Revolutionary Freedom Movement says, "Only when we have reclaimed our homeland by force can Jews, Christians, and Moslems live in peace
there," and the children have no cause for skepticism. These
children, who have suffered terribly under Zionist wars of conquest, will seize every chance to do their part in freeing their
people from suffering and oppression. Western reporters emphasize military drill in the camps but ignore the main thrust of the
Freedom Movement — the attempt to tell the children the history
of their own people and of their neighbors, to teach them the
meaning of their present fight as part of the international struggle
of the proletariat, and, through discussion, theater, and games,
criticism and self-criticism, to liberate them and make them politically conscious human beings.

The magazine *Pardon* became interested in the Black Panthers'

efforts in the United States to educate their children in Liberation
Schools. *Pardon* interviewed one school's founder (issue 2, Feb.
1970) and we reprint the article here without commentary:

*Black children in white schools learn nothing about class con-
flicts in North American society, because these schools systematically train them to do nothing towards changing this society.
For this reason, the Black Panther Party has started Liberation
Schools all over the United States. In small, dirty rooms off back
alleys and in store fronts about 40,000 black children are meeting
during their vacations from ordinary schools and learning to understand why their fathers demonstrate and agitate, why they
want to break the chains with which the white man has bound
them.*

*Pardon located one of these free schools. In Queens, a New York
City borough synonymous with the comfortable middle class life,
the sort of life from which its black citizens are excluded, over
80 students ranging from the ages of 2 to 16 (the majority between
9 and 13) are learning the things schools don't usually teach. We
talked to Deputy Captain Carlton Yearwood, founder of this
Liberation School:*

*Pardon: How many Liberation Schools are there now in the
U.S.A.?*

*Yearwood: Almost every cell of the Black Panther Party runs
one. In New York, we already have around eight.*

Pardon: Do the Liberation Schools have a set program?

*Yearwood: Yes. The children learn to read, but on a new level.
They learn to read newspapers and books that clarify certain
topics, in contrast to books like* Little Dog Jeff *or* Jack and Jill.
We use Dying Colonialism *by Frantz Fanon;* Soul on Ice *by
Eldridge Cleaver;* The Diary of Che Guevara; *Mao's "Red Book";*
The United Front Against Fascism *by Georgi Dimitrov; and Huey
Newton's* Essays. *While they learn to read, they simultaneously
learn to recognize the contradictions in this society and to become young revolutionaries. Their reading improves daily, for
reading is a tool of survival, a tool that teaches them how to
change this society; they learn how one might begin to build a
new society, one that would feed ALL people and house and
clothe them like human beings.*

*Pardon: Do you give the children a completely nonrepressive
kind of education, or is there a certain amount of discipline?*

Yearwood: We use a certain amount of discipline, but on

Maoist-Leninist principles, which say that criticism strengthens the community. If a student has some criticism to make during a lesson, the debate between student and teacher continues until one or the other is persuaded. For agreement on a theoretical level means unity in action. Only then does the lesson continue.

We also teach the children not to be racist. Many blacks still have racist attitudes. We teach the children that the basic problem in America is not racism itself, but the oppression and exploitation in a capitalist system which creates racist tendencies. The needs of an early stage of capitalism brought blacks into this country. For hundreds of years, the capitalists have encouraged racist attitudes in both poor blacks and poor whites, so that they would not realize they had a common enemy. So we have explained to the children that blacks are racist towards blacks of a different class and that whites are racist towards other whites for the same reason. Already, the children identify with the slogan ALL POWER TO THE PEOPLE and know what it means. This, I believe, is the greatest triumph of the Liberation School.

Pardon: Were there problems with parents?

Yearwood: No.

Pardon: And with officials?

Yearwood: There were the usual problems and hassles with the pig-bureaucrats. Three of our teachers, for instance, were arrested on some pretext. That's the usual procedure. But it didn't work because the kids came and they're still coming. New teachers took over till the others got out of prison.

Pardon: What was the pretext used to arrest the teachers?

Yearwood: Possession of dangerous weapons and so forth. But as soon as the Liberation School term was over, they dropped the charges.

Pardon: Doesn't the effect of the Liberation School experience disappear when vacation is over and the kids go back to their usual schools?

Yearwood: The effect lasts, because the kids still come to our Party office and are taught there according to revolutionary belief. We've learned from parents about the effects of our training: six- and seven-year-old kids have criticized their teacher for the kind of instruction they were getting in the ordinary school. They wanted to read Eldridge Cleaver instead of Jack and Jill. We're going to set up another school soon in Queens, to be open year round on afternoons and weekends.

Pardon: What's been the effect of the Liberation School on

its students — comparing them to other black children?

Yearwood: The kids have been telling the others they should come and get a different kind of education than they get in public school. The other day there was a trip from the public school to the Statue of Liberty, and the teacher got criticized for what goes on in our society. "If you don't think the Statue of Liberty means anything," she said, "what would you set up in its place?" One of our kids gave her an answer, "A statue of Huey P. Newton."

In our society, the spectre of political indoctrination inevitably looms up in connection with the liberation movements of the third world, the American Black Power movement, and the Socialist Day Care Centers. Political slogans coming out of children's mouths cause subliminal recall of horrible episodes in German history. The crucial error lies in fearfully avoiding any political education for children and swallowing the myth of an idyllic childhood in the bosom of the family, a myth which just favors reactionary indoctrination.

You don't fight fascism by insidiously instilling in children obedience and passive acceptance of capitalism. Instead, as early as possible, we must try to show children the blatantly obvious contradictions in this capitalist system and the connection between the anticapitalist liberation struggle in the third world and the class struggle at home.

There is a difference between children carrying flags because a leader told them to — as when, for instance, some statesman (like Nixon) is touring and they get the day off from school (the reasons for this statesman's friendship with their government being quite incomprehensible to them) — and children carrying a flag that relates to their existence, one that means resistance to known oppression, e.g., in school.

What did political education in the Berlin Storefront Day Care Centers amount to? First, we must say that there was no general agreement on the subject. None of the centers offered formal political instruction; none systematically taught the children political slogans, verses, or things like that. We did share a basic concept of political education for preschoolers: we tried to explain, in a political way, social conflicts in which the children became involved (e.g., confrontations with landlords, superintendents, and police), showing that these were conflicts between interest groups that are privileged in our society and others that are oppressed.

We tried to make the children aware of social conflicts as

these impinged directly on their lives; and we tried especially to generalize and make objective the meaning of these conflicts. (One does not tell children that police are "bad" or "good," but one does explain that they have certain functions — to direct traffic, to beat up demonstrators, to help children who have gotten lost.)

Our children also get part of their political education through participation in adult political activity: they help distribute flyers; they attend teach-ins, demonstrations, etc. Naturally, the children have invented political games — "demonstration," "tenants-against-landlords," "Vietnam" (stimulated by the pictures and posters around their homes). Three- and four-year-olds can easily grasp arguments and logical connections when they are put in terms a child can understand. No wonder, then, the children have always identified with the National Liberation Front and not the American aggressors.

From its inception, the Schöneberg center emphasized political education and made specific recommendations in that area:

The center must not define its job as nothing more than education. We must understand that our work involves just the first stage in what will be a lifetime of critical awareness. More important, the center must see that its work falls within the political perspective of the left wing movement. The further growth of the centers, in fact their very survival, depends entirely on the expansion of the socialist movement. Therefore the centers cannot have a purely psychoanalytic orientation; they must also concern themselves with social and political factors. Education in the centers cannot be neutral. It must be political. Simply teaching people about the concept of "sexual freedom" will not release them from the authoritarian personality structure which our society imposes.

Education to and through political action is the most useful type of political education. Preschoolers can be involved through play, through instruction, and through work in which they can share.

Children's theater has a great potential for stimulating the children. . . . They should be given a chance to act out scenes in their lives, scenes of oppression and successful resistance. Marionettes and puppets can be preludes to individual role playing. This kind of theater is particularly suitable for "caricaturing social and political confrontations." Police, school, and church can be effectively simplified; and the relationship

between *capitalist* and *worker, worker* and *farmer, soldier* and
proletariat can be portrayed in striking stereotypes.
—Hörnle, *Education and Class Struggle,* preface to Central Council
    pamphlet no. 3, pp. v. ff. Cf. literature in appendix

Founding the Central Council

In June, three Storefront Day Care Centers were in operation,
one in Neukölln and two in Schöneberg. (The Schöneberg center
had split into two groups because the older and younger children
got in each other's way.) More centers were being organized in
Charlottenburg, Lichterfelde, Steglitz, and Wilmersdorf.

This was the time when grave problems first arose in the
Action Council, problems connected with our ongoing theoretical
and organizational work. The women involved in planning the
new centers and working in the task forces began to miss more
and more of the Wednesday plenary meetings of those interested
in the centers. This was due partly to the fact that the task forces
hadn't yet completed any reports to present at the plenary, and
partly to the arrival of so many newcomers at the Wednesday
meetings, which made focused discussion impossible.

We tried to solve this, unsuccessfully, by involving newcomers
in the task forces and having only delegates from these groups
come to the general meeting. Because of defective organization,
the political image the Action Council had hoped to project
clearly was not realized.

Meanwhile, the centers had attracted the interest of the Senate
and the public. It became necessary to formulate some policy
on publicity and to work out a strategy which would ensure that
our original political aims in nonauthoritarian education did not
vanish into individual artisanship. It was also imperative to find
some way for the different centers to exchange information about
their experiences and learn from each other. Since the Action
Council couldn't take on this job, the Lichterfeld center took the
initiative and called a Central Council of Socialist Day Care
Centers of West Berlin on October 8, 1968.

Everyone agreed, first, to a general embargo on information to
the mass media in order to stop the false reports and slanderous
descriptions. At that time it was not possible to issue definitive
reports about the centers, but we decided to publish our own
pamphlets later on, and we printed an INFO sheet for the use of

those working in the centers (see, for example, Documents, p. 94). The Schöneberg center had tried to get Senate support without relinquishing control of the center to officials of the regional bureaucracy. Officialdom was hard pressed to fit the new institution into the old regulations. They had trouble deciding whether to call the center a "Children's Home" or a "Day Care Center," because neither label quite fit. The success of applications filed by other centers, following the Schöneberg example, will depend on the good will of individual officials. But at the time of this writing, only the Schöneberg and Friednau centers had managed to get Senate support. In the Central Council, discussion about getting Senate assistance naturally led to discussion of the political position of the centers in general. While some centers thought they should do no more than babysit, most viewed their work as a promising step in revolutionary organization.

   The story of the Central Council, in our opinion, exemplifies a tendency that will dominate the attempts of future socialist movements to connect political goals and the organization of groups to achieve them. The movement, in its effort to reach the masses, must identify with the immediate interests, wishes, and hopes of the people. This means that those realms which are now considered private must be drawn into political work. . . . Our job is to consciously liberate and organize the existing trends in social behavior to collective life and work. We already know from our experience in the centers that at the times when the collective was felt to be a relatively secure place, some energies previously bound up in suppressing unconscious fears were made available for political work.
   But this process is not automatic. The beginnings of community organization in areas previously thought of as strictly private always risk cooptation. The danger can be avoided only if these self-organized groups include politically conscious members who continually remind everyone of their relationship to the larger societal situation. The Central Council of Socialist Day Care Centers of West Berlin defines itself, therefore, as part of the socialist movement. Its task will be to go from the self-help efforts of active Leftists to the initiation of self-help organizations among the mass of wage earners. However, only a few people in the center task forces are ready to undertake this work; most of them, especially the women, must first go further in their own psychological and

*political emancipation, so that they can free their energies for this
task.*

— Preface to Central Council Pamphlet #1,
Vera Schmidt, Three Essays, Berlin, 1969

Further Work with the Action Council

Only a minority of women had clear political motives when they
entered the Action Council of Women's Liberation. Many were
motivated by the experience of being personally oppressed in the
family and at their work, for instance, in student life. Most, it is
true, had passed the stage of thinking their problems were entirely
their own fault and were aware of the social causes behind them
— but almost all were totally confused about how political organization could be used to combat these difficulties.

Organizing the nursery at the Vietnam Conference or working
in the Day Care Centers, for most women the first experience of
collective action, only brought their concepts of collective organization to a certain point. The personal isolation which previously
had made most of the women incapable of any attempt at cooperative theoretical work could only slowly be overcome. The women
decided, therefore, to explain their problems to SDS, hoping to get
some help in solving their organizational difficulties. At the SDS
conference in Frankfurt, one woman ran a workshop, attended by
women from various cities, and the group drew up a resolution
(see Documents, pp. 23 ff.).

Since SDS, as we mentioned previously, could not solve its own
organizational problems, and since the troubles of the women in
the workshop stemmed not from a lack of organizational ability
but from erroneous theoretical assumptions, the assistance given
by SDS women did not prove to be of much practical value, although some of them did join the Action Council. The newcomers
created problems in the Council about authority, a difficulty which
their previous experience in SDS certainly hadn't remedied. In
order to speak at all, they had been forced to identify with the
male authorities and they found that they couldn't easily enter a
specifically female solidarity. The conflicts were analogous to
those of the bourgeois career woman, constantly glamorized in
women's magazines as an example of "the emancipated female."

The Action Council held an informational meeting in October
for all the new women and arranged for an office where the West
German members could get answers to any questions they might

have and obtain an up-to-date list of existing Day Care Centers and Women's Workshops. Several progress reports were issued, which attempted to draw general conclusions from previous experience and to set forth some clear political guidelines; bibliographies for those interested in theoretical work were compiled and distributed (see Documents, pp. 33 ff.). In conjunction with the two Charlottenburg centers, the Action Council in November put out a flyer, calling "all active workers in the Socialist Day Care Centers" to a meeting at the Technical University. There, urgent problems were to be discussed and the bond between the centers and the Action Council was to be revitalized. But the meeting turned out to be quite chaotic and did not get us any nearer to finding solutions. Thereafter, individuals used their energies in study groups concerned with specific subjects.

Documents B

The First Public Reactions

How the Storefront Day Care Centers Were Described and
Slandered in the Senate and the Press

The Press Attacks Senate

**NO DAY CARE FACILITIES FOR 18,000 CHILDREN
ARE BLUE LETTERS THE ANSWER?**

The Senator for Family, Youth, and Sport gives new hope for solving one of
the major problems in West Berlin. An attempt will be made to borrow some
crumbs from the middle class to relieve the startling shortage of Day Care.
Existing institutions now have over 18,000 children on waiting lists.

Some districts are using "blue letters" to try to make room for especially
needy children. If a family is earning too much, their child is asked to leave.
A rather "unfortunate situation," agrees the Senate department responsible.
Anyway, a solution like this is just a drop in the bucket. It does, however, offer
some help to mothers without husbands and to very low income families.

Strict Selectivity
Obviously, Day Care Centers are not yet expelling children right and left.
In Schöneberg, for example, 27 notices were issued. Says City Councilor
Kettner: "The children can stay until June 1. We also offered them the option
of a half-day schedule. In the future we will be much more selective about
admissions. But the fact remains that for every child admitted, another one is
waiting." No clear guidelines based on income have been set. If there are
pressing education problems, even a "poor little rich child" can stay. Neukölln
likewise is trying to review its policies. Again it seems unwise to set an arbitrary

maximum income cut-off point. Even for a high income family which had just taken on heavy financial commitments, a notice of expulsion might mean excessive hardship.

Review of Pupils in Neukölln

About 50 students are being weeded out in Neukölln to make room for the children whose mothers either live alone or are forced to supplement their husbands' income. Another way to ease the pressure may be to have the older children go after school to a children's home, where they could play under supervision until their parents pick them up.

In almost every district, people have just one question: if the big companies really want female workers, why won't they set up enough Day Care Centers close to factories and offices? Admittedly, the average Day Care Center does cost about a million marks ($250,000).

Despite the demand, West German factories and businesses have started very few Day Care Centers. So far six companies can offer 297 places in their day care centers. Centers attached to a group of six hospitals account for another 319 places. Five more Day Care Centers for 399 children are planned — but only the hospitals are involved here.

The idea that centers should be built in the area where the mother works developed after the Wall was built in 1961. Western industry urgently needed female workers to replace those who could no longer cross over from East Berlin. Due to those conditions, the Senate's Department for Youth and Sport began negotiations with the companies. But what the companies offered didn't quite suit the Senate. The companies were willing to subsidize Day Care Centers only if a set number of places were reserved for them. The offer was rejected because it meant that some places would regularly be kept empty. The companies wanted them reserved, empty or not.

A company in Zehlendorf recently made a different offer. They will provide buildings if the district will provide personnel. But this will probably come to nothing because the government has limited plans for staff increases.

Private companies are as gloomy and suspicious as the Department for Youth and Sport is delighted at each and every extra Day Care Center place. Since mothers generally don't live close to their place of work, the children would have to get up very early to go to nurseries with them. They would have to be subjected to the daily experience of rush hour traffic. Since most children attend a school somewhere near their homes, those old enough for school would also face the hardship of a daily shuttle from school to center back to home.

Another possibility exists, however: several firms in one area could jointly build a center and take any children who lived in that area.

IN THE LAND OF FRIEDRICH FRÖBEL, NO ROOM FOR CHILDREN
Berlin Day Care Center Plans Have Not Succeeded

A pleasant picture: children playing in sandboxes, sunshine, a friendly and energetic lady hovers over them. Any mother can rest assured that her child is in good hands in a Day Care Center. But not every mother can send her child to a center: there is not enough room. Yet centers today aren't just for children whose mothers must work to help out the family. More and more mothers want to have a career even though they don't need the money. Educators believe, moreover, that the experience of a Day Care Center is generally best for the small child.

At the end of 1966 there were about 308,000 children under 15 in West Berlin. For these children, some centers exist and more are being built. Centers usually have three separate areas: a crib area for children under 3, the kindergarten for children from 3 to 6, and another area for school children up to 15. The 6- to 15-year-olds are the largest group (160,000) but they are not the largest group in the centers. Kindergarten children are. At the end of 1966 there were 71,500 children in Berlin of kindergarten age, as well as 76,500 children under 3 who could theoretically be cared for in cribs.

Plans by the Senate Department for Youth and Sport are based on the assumption that *there should be enough centers to accommodate 15 percent of the children under 15.* But success is by no means in sight. There are places for only 9.7 percent now. Practically all the centers have long waiting lists; this alone shows that there is still a great need. About 10,000 children are on the lists, and many parents don't bother to register their children because there is so little chance of getting in.

West Berlin now has 227 public Day Care Centers with 20,588 places and 216 private centers, some church-connected, with 11,527 places. (The ten private company kindergartens with a total of 550 places hardly make much difference.) At this time, over half the places are assigned to kindergarten children. The Senate plans to increase the percentage. When the goal of places for 15 percent of the children is reached, the distribution will be: 5 percent for crib children, 75 percent for kindergarten children, 17 percent for school children, and 3 percent for special groups including the handicapped. But no one will predict when exactly all this will come about. Of the twelve districts in Berlin, only Tiergarten has reached the 15 percent figure. But in that district, it is already clear that 15 percent won't do.

Only a few years ago, Berlin planned Day Care Centers using a 10 percent figure. The planners, realizing the figure was far too low, raised the percentage to 15. On the basis of that figure, the city bought or reserved various plots of land on which to build centers. The plans take into consideration the different needs of different districts. On the average, the plans allow about 3,600 square yards for 141 children.

But the idea is not to cover Berlin with a network of Day Care Centers. There are plans now before the Senate for multipurpose structures which would house clubs for the elderly, clinics or youth centers, as well as Day Care Centers. There is also talk of starting supervised playgrounds with a shelter for bad weather. These would be far cheaper than Day Care Centers.

According to a recent study by the Senate Department for Youth and Sport, these are the major criteria for admission to a Day Care Center: in 91.5 percent of the cases, the fact that the mother worked; 0.6 percent of the children were referred by the Children's Counselling Service and 3.5 percent by family welfare agencies. Only 4.4 percent were admitted for "other reasons." This group includes children whose parents, although the mother doesn't work, think their child would benefit from getting acquainted with his peers.

A look at other countries — not just at Eastern Europe — shows that the land of kindergartens now lags far behind. (Friedrich Fröbel (1782–1852), a German teacher, devoted his life to preschool education and is called the "father of the kindergarten." He founded the first kindergarten in Blankenburg, Thur, in 1840.) Comparisons are misleading, however, because some countries have compulsory preschool education in the elementary schools and thus appear to have very few kindergartens. More and more German education experts recommend a system of compulsory preschool education, which, if implemented, would demand a vastly more extensive kindergarten arrangement.

Act One: The Senator for Family, Youth, and Sport Welcomes the Storefront Day Care Centers

A letter from the Senator for Family, Youth, and Sport (29.11.68)

Dear Dr. Wolff: Thank you for your detailed letter of 6.11.68; your educational theory interested me very much. I agree with you that fostering the family as the "basic unit of the state" implies not in the least an orientation to democratic methods of child rearing. Such an approach should keep in mind predictions on the effect of present social trends on the character of marriage and the family. I find the Storefront Day Care Centers, which began through your initiative, remarkable in just this respect, for they offer a model of the civic functioning of the family, and I would, therefore, like to aid them financially, beginning in 1969.

Considering the varied structure of your different Storefront Centers and their varying worth as models, they should clearly be considered individually for differential financial support, and this process will require further discussion.

As a precondition, unpaid cooperative work by parents would have to continue and would have to continue to maintain a connection with efforts to explore educational theory.

For further discussion with the administration, I suggest you see the head of Department II, Dr. Arno F. Kosmale, who will be able to discuss the matter with you.

Yours respectfully,

Horst Korber

Act Two: The Press Ambushes the Storefront Centers

Since we did have some idea of what came next, the Central Council decided to impose an embargo on information to the press. We thoroughly explained the reasons and most, but unfortunately not all, of our members upheld it. So this appeared in *Storefront Day Care Centers #2:*

On the Bourgeois Press

A few reasons not to let them use you:

First, most of the bourgeois and liberal news reporters are in no position to understand our work. We know from our own case that just reading — for instance, Vera Schmidt — is not enough, and that our self-awareness comes mainly from concrete experience.

Second, publication. Why would anyone, if he did understand our work, want to write about it in the popular press? News is a commodity, and it is brought to the market as such. The issue isn't what the news says but whether it sells. (The best news would be tales of sex orgies in the Storefronts.) Our understanding of the political nature of daily life, our view of the conflicts which the nuclear family soon suppresses in most children, our struggle to permit open expression of the conflicts — these won't sell. Information on the centers, therefore, will necessarily be reduced to what will sell. Consequently, the articles can include nothing we would consider important.

Two examples: "Sexual activity was not prohibited; adults concerned themselves only with why it had occurred" (*Taggesspiegel*). And, "In all probability, the Treasury of the State will not approve this application for funds as in the public interest. It has been reported that children are allowed to bash each other's heads in with wooden blocks, and this is not generally understood to be in the public interest" (*Morgenpost*).

On having the press get our approval before printing an article: as far as we know, our work serves no vested interest, but that is what counts in getting newspapers to print what you want. One need only consider the past experience of the Left with such pledges. These people have had years to cultivate a vast repertoire of tricks in reporting opinions and distorting information, ideas, and statements. Since it would take us forever to catch up, it would be a waste of energy; even then we might lose, because they own the means of production. We can win only by doing the writing and publishing ourselves.

Let's face it: they will try bribery. Right now, Storefront Day Care Centers have a high market value. And information will be paid for. Once the market is glutted, of course, interest will wane. But the sums the papers offer are so ridiculous that disregarding past experience and selling an interview to them isn't worth the nausea next morning when you see what they made of your conversation.

The habit of setting only short-term goals and stressing rationality in reaching them; materialism adapted to a world dominated by business, work, consumerism; stunting of the instincts, failure or renunciation of the effort to sublimate, and an ensuing inability to learn — all obvious in the proletariat — are made possible by negating the needs of the individual. And the pressures which deform the parental personality crush the children into the same mold.

Hence, the first steps in educating the proletariat must be a united struggle to satisfy basic needs, the effort to see through the false satisfactions and false sublimations offered by bourgeois society and bourgeois education. It is essential to help people begin to recognize their real needs and the real forms of satisfaction and sublimation, to find types of productive work. Proletarian education does not mean forced collectivization, as in the kibbutz; it does not mean renunciation of individuality; it does not mean conformism, but the opposite. Our ideas of needs and productive capacities are to be specifically and consciously adapted to the individual case. Solidarity is the fighting stance which permits us to begin to recognize and fulfill our needs as individuals.

In January the attack began in earnest, with Springer at the head of the pack.

(1) Young Berlin parents are trying to start model kindergartens. What's the idea? Private preschools run by the parents. On private initiative, almost a hundred of these "Storefront Day Care Centers" have sprung up in our city in the last year. Has this experiment got a future? The Senate thinks so. Twelve of the new schools are going to serve as models for the city — the Senate proposes to give them money. But nobody's sure that the parents will "play ball."

In the Storefront Day Care Centers, Mao Ousts Little Red Riding Hood

Young Parents Want Nonauthoritarian Education for Aggression
"Is there really a kindergarten here?" was the surprised response of everyone I met in the gleaming hallways of the office building in the Jebenstrasse.

Finally, on the top floor, I found a door without the standard business plaque and which had a key hanging beside it for anyone to use. This is the first Day Care Center which the students started.

The aim here is education for aggression to create "antiauthoritarian" individuals. The children are to be "shaped" so that they can fulfill their parents' wishes for a "better" future generation.

Unusual Decor

"What's she doing here?" shrieked a child when I came in. With some difficulty, I waded through knee-high piles of foamrubber chips and took in the unusual kindergarten decor. There were red banners hanging from the ceiling and posters of Mao and Che on the walls. But the children's own wall painting is even brighter and more explosive, for these children are allowed to run wild.

The furnishings are rather shabby, the garbage pail in the tiny kitchen is overflowing, and the smell of stale food and dirty children is suffocating.

Two young mothers sit calmly among little children busily smashing with hammers whatever strikes their fancy.

Conversations with parents in the Neukölln and Steglitz centers brought out quite clearly two of their main ideas:

1. They think traditional kindergartens stifle the individuality and budding critical spirit of the young. As proof, they say that no kindergarten teacher can really give fifteen children individual care. (In the centers, there are only eight to ten children in a group, and two parents usually help.) Also, traditional kindergartens are saturated with the educational methods of a "hypocritical society."

2. The direction of education is to be decided by discussion in a parents' collective.

"Anyone who won't bow to the group gets thrown out." This means that the kindergarten teacher — and the parents often find they can't do without one — must attend the frequent evening discussions.

The parents had nothing to say about preparing their children for school, for they still haven't decided what to do about that. Some children, however, are now five and will soon be going to school.

Parents Don't Worry

The parents don't worry about their children's future encounters with other children, differently raised, and with other kinds of teachers. "By the time they're six, our children will have such strong personalities," said one parent confidently, "that they can handle such things easily."

The parents also intend to start their own schools, "where we can apply our ideas to learning the ABC."

They deny indignantly the accusation that they are using their children as guinea pigs: "If you've seen the public kindergartens, you know that anything we do is sure to be an improvement."

In the matter of education, the parents have not limited themselves to opposing traditional education; they have other specific goals. "We want our children to learn to be aggressive early, so that they will from an early age rise up fearlessly against the existing order."

Against the Senate

In Berlin, the children's aggression will ultimately be directed against the Senate: "We must set a good example for our children," these parents say. So far, few have had any dealings with the local government. Any contacts that have been made, as in Neukölln, Charlottenburg, Steglitz, and Schöneberg, have been to demand money.

The local government of Charlottenburg helped two centers, in the Hehenstauffenstrasse and Sieglindenstrasse, to overcome their chronic poverty. It made two special grants of 500 DM and 750 DM, in addition to allocating a regular monthly subsidy. All other district governments refused support, even when, as in Neukölln, the parents threatened "drastic action."

One father had only this comment on the Senate's decision to give support: "We haven't decided yet whether we want to be used by the Senate, maybe even to be advertised as proof of benevolence. If we agree to accept support, we will have to be absolutely sure our freedom is not compromised."

They aren't worried about the future of their Storefronts. In under one year, over a 100 centers have appeared in West Berlin. "Don't you think we can find other empty rooms?"

— Ursula Gröttrup

(2) VALUABLE EXPERIMENTS, SAYS THE SENATE

Are the Storefront Day Care Centers worthwhile? The Senate answers with an emphatic yes. "We find these attempts most interesting. Perhaps these models can give valuable ideas to our public day care centers."

There's no denying the commitment of the young people who founded the Storefronts. The Senate recognizes this. The young parents not only spend time looking for places to rent but renovate and furnish them as well. In order to do their share of the work some mothers have even changed from full- to part-time jobs, because one of the fundamental principles held by these private kindergartens is that all parents should take an active part in the education of their children.

The idea that all parents take part in the work means, in practice, that different mothers and fathers take charge of the children on different days. Hence, in contrast to traditional kindergartens, these have no one "caretaker." In the evenings the parents discuss the problems of child raising as they come up and try to agree on a consistent approach.

So far this has not always worked. As a result various groups have split up or broken up altogether. And it frequently happens that their educational theories cannot be applied.

Despite these difficulties, the Senate hopes to gain, through work with some of these centers, stimulating ideas for developing its own preschool program.

If, at the beginning of next year, the Senate names about twelve of these centers as educational "models," it is to foster a spirit of working cooperation. Financial support from the Senate Department for Family, Youth, and Sport is meant to ensure that the Storefront Centers continue — as educational models.

So far, however, it is unclear how much money will be given or for what purposes. "In this matter, we want to do things on an individual basis," says the current Senator.

It remains to be seen whether the young parents will agree to the conditions set by the Senate Department for Family, Youth, and Sport. For there is still antagonism between the Senate, open to the experiment, and the center parents. Few of the latter are prepared to work in official cooperation with the government.

In many centers education is apparently confused with political indoctrination. The Senate will definitely have to put in a great deal of work in order to achieve its own purposes in the Storefront experiment.

— LUK

Stern reveals all:

*The little leftist
children stick their bare hands in
paint pots and spatter the peeling
wallpaper at the Berlin "Storefront Day
Care Centers." They stick out their tongues
at visitors and play Vietnam War. They sing "Ring
Around the Rosy" and "The Internationale."
No prohibitions, no punishments for them.
Their parents call it the education
of the future.*

Little Leftists with Big Rights — the Berlin Extra-Parliamentary Opposition (APO) is experimenting with their children. They have founded twelve non-repressive Storefront Centers where children aren't compelled to do anything.

The kindergarten teacher, bearded and wearing a fur cap, belongs to SEW, (Western Socialist Unity party), as the SED (German Socialist Unity party) of West Berlin has been calling itself lately. His name is Jim Kruse. Jim Kruse is reading "Extra-Dienst," the APO newspaper. Around him, children are putting potties on each other's heads as helmets. One little boy is smearing mashed bananas into a little girl's hair. Another repeatedly crashes his tricycle into the

wall. The wall is in the process of being decorated, not by painters, but by children sticking their bare hands in a pot of paint and spattering the peeling wallpaper.

This doesn't ruffle Jim Kruse. He's reading about the latest actions of the APO. Only when his two-and-a-half-year-old daughter Anna nudges him does he look up and ask her, "Do you have to shit?" Anna nods. He pulls down her pants and sits her on the potty.

It's Jim Kruse's day to work in the "nonauthoritarian" kindergarten in Neukölln, one of the twelve in West Berlin in which the children of the Left get together to play.

The first left wing kindergarten was organized at the Vietnam Conference at the Technical University last year as an emergency solution to the dilemma of mothers who wanted to go to demonstrations and march in the streets. The experiment was such a success that the "Action Council of Women's Liberation," whose members consider themselves oppressed by the male sex, decided that for the time being they should work to liberate themselves from their own children.

For the APO, public and church kindergartens were out of the question, because many parents believed that their own hang-ups came from an overly authoritarian education in precisely such institutions. Some of the parents, very involved in studying the Russian Revolution and its consequences, had read about the Moscow psychologist Vera Schmidt. A "Child Care Laboratory" was founded in 1921 by Vera Schmidt. Even at that time, she wanted child raising to be nonauthoritarian and without sexual taboos.

Caroline Asks About "Bad Cops"

Armed with Vera Schmidt's book, the APO parents founded a "Central Council of the Storefront Day Care Centers." They rented vacant store fronts (hence the name) and put in imaginatively painted old furniture. The parents hoped that by taking turns in the centers they could avoid hiring an orthodox, authoritarian teacher, and save money as well.

There was great enthusiasm at the Central Council's first meeting — "We are the start of a major breakthrough." Even a few professional educators agreed. Anne-Marie Tausch, using tapes, had already researched the problems of traditional kindergartens in terms of the needs of a democracy. Eighty-two percent of what teachers in public kindergartens say to their charges consists of commands like "Sit still," "Wipe your nose," "Go away," "Shut up."

Words like these, according to the believers in nonrepressive education, create the "ass-kissers" of the future. But even education which doesn't put a premium on sitting still and wiping your nose has problems. Jim Kruse vouches for that: "The Day Care Center is a big pile of shit. It only keeps going because we have to have somewhere to put our children. But you really can't call it collective education."

It doesn't take long to see that the centers still haven't reached great heights. In Neukölln, in the basement of a shabby apartment house in the working class district near Rollberg, the furnace stops when it drops below freezing outside. Almost all the children have coughs. In the kitchen, there are stacks of dirty dishes, garbage, and soiled diapers. The feeling of life on a barge. Capitalist figures like Mr. Clean are locked out of the Neukölln center.

Jim Kruse sees signs of progress, however. "We don't stop our children masturbating and we let them play sex games in peace. Many children were already toilet-trained. Now they shit in their pants again. They're repeating the anal phase* and that's good. Did you know that most concentration camp guards had trouble with toilet-training?"

Jim Kruse and his friends had clear political reasons for going into the workers' quarter of Neukölln. They wanted to raise their children with workers' children to build, at last, a real link with the working classes. "Politically we're a failure. The workers would rather send their children to public kindergartens. Our place is too dirty for them." Workers also, as he admitted, place particular value on obedience in children.

Obedience is not a goal of the APO centers. For instance, take Caroline, a four-year-old who attends the center in the Sieglindestrasse. When Caroline sees a policeman in the street she runs up to him and asks, "Are you a bad cop?" The question is not accidental — her mother, Dietlind Kruger (31), has had ample opportunity to get acquainted with police clubs, most recently on the second day of Christmas when demonstrators stormed the abandoned building of the Chinese military mission in West Berlin. Dietlind Kruger, a believer in the "militant Left," is separated from her husband, a radio reporter. As she herself is eager to admit, she owes her hang-ups to a repressive upbringing.

She wants her three daughters to have a better chance. They are to have only a nonrepressive education. Sabine (12) is often away for days. A few weeks ago Dietlind took Katherine (10) out of school because the teacher was too authoritarian. She will send her to school in East Germany. And Dietlind Kruger goes with her youngest to the Storefront Center.

"The hardest part is to get the children to take a midday nap without being authoritarian," she says. She proudly reports the group spirit which the children in the Sieglindestrasse have developed in such a short time. "Children who have played together all day are allowed to go home together at night and sleep together."

---

* Psychoanalysis refers to an "anal stage" in early childhood as marking a phase of sexual development when excretion produces feelings of pleasure.

For an amateur kindergarten teacher, Mrs. Kruger has big plans: "We want to develop a children's collective, which can be sent into the schools as a kind of advance regiment. They'll give the authoritarian teachers quite a time." When Dietlind Kruger works at the center, she plays "Ring Around the Rosy" with the nine children, but she also sings the "Internationale" with them. The children play train with bureau drawers. But they also like "capitalist toys" from West Berlin stores, where the radical parents break windows periodically.

A popular game in the Sieglindestrasse is to stand at the front window and stick your tongue out at passers-by or give them the finger. At the Schützenstrasse the little children can use matches to light the stove, play with scissors and other sharp objects and, swinging from a rope attached to the ceiling, sail six feet above the floor. A good bourgeois piano used to be part of the furniture, but the revolutionary progeny tested it so hard that it gave up every last note.

In all the centers the parents meet weekly to work out menus and assign supervision days. Written notes, kept on every child, are discussed at these meetings.

One example: the three-year-old twins Henrietta and Fabian, children of APO member Henry Schiffer, stood out from the group. Fabian was always throwing things around the place. Henrietta always wanted to climb into the baby carriage and suck her thumb. The next meeting amounted to a trial of the Schiffers. Their comrades asked them if they had difficulty reaching orgasm, or why else would their children be so aggressive? The couple began to discuss intimate details of their life in front of the group.

Frau Schiffer on her husband: "He doesn't care, except theoretically, about raising children. He just hands me books and I don't understand them. We can't have a washing machine because he doesn't want to give in to consumerism." Herr Schiffer on his wife: "When I come home she's just sitting there mending her old bras. She should send the laundry to her mother."

When someone interrupted to point out that this was irrational, Schiffer ended all discussion by screaming, "You Stalinist shithead!"

Despite such troubles, the parents of the Sieglindestrasse center are reproached by other parents for having such an easy life. For even one Senate official sends his child there. The district actually subsidizes this center. And the place is cleaned regularly.

Dr. Oeckel, medical district supervisor, didn't find that life was so "easy" in the Hohenstauffenstrasse center which she visited last November. At the end of her report, she added: "During our visit, she (the mother in charge) was unable to take care of the five children or to prevent them from using our heads as targets in their ball game." Some children emptied boxes of toys on the doctor's head, others tried to spit on her. "They also tried," according to the report, "to drill holes in our heads with some sort of corkscrew device."

Wife Swapping as an Educational Device

Meanwhile things got to be too much for the Hohenstauffenstrasse parents. Like many other Storefront Centers, they hired a kindergarten teacher trained by the state institutions in authoritarian child raising.

Jochen Rebbein, father of a child raised in the nonauthoritarian manner until that time, explained the retrogression to hiring a teacher — "The parents decided not to let the children have their own way about everything any more. Some things are prohibited now — they have to respect property. They were too destructive before.

"Instead the men began swapping wives because, according to one participant, children shouldn't be fixated on a single couple." But the Hohenstauffenstrasse parents didn't find that helped much, and they gave up wife swapping.

Charlottenburg 1 has the strictest ideology. Commune 2 runs the show there. Thus the sculptor Heinrich Brumack and his son Marcus were expelled, although he had done a great deal of work in fixing up the place. "As an artist you have individual, not collective, work experience."

At this center a five-year-old boy took a three-year-old girl to the toilet and undressed her. He injured her during their sex play. The girl's mother, when she removed her child from the center, was mercilessly accused of "petit bourgeois sentimentality." And the boy's parents complained because "the boy was cheated of his pleasure-object."

Recently a Berlin citizen, Helga Henckel, had a shocking experience with an APO child. In a letter to the newspaper *Die Zeit*, she quoted his description of a day at the Storefront Center: "We played Vietnam today and we shot lots of Americans dead."

Meanwhile, the Senate is planning to give 50,000 DM to four of these centers. But the Central Council wants all the centers to share the money. Therefore no agreement has been reached. Arnim Tschoepe, who runs a group studying the civic functioning of the family in the office of the Senator for Family, Youth, and Sport admits: "Public education does not do justice to the demands of educational science. The centers serve as interesting models of civic functioning of the family."

The Senate thus wishes to study the type of child raising done by those it habitually drives off the streets with riot sticks. Those who habitually get beaten up want financial support for their child raising programs from the same people they usually demonstrate against.

The psychiatrist Dr. Gunther Ammon, who has treated many APO people who want to regain their emotional health, has more suspicions about the Storefront Centers than the Senate does. His reproach: "The Left should straighten out their own complexes rather than tinker with their children. All the red princes and princesses want is to dispose of their children. And as usual, the whole thing is ideologically camouflaged." Dr. Ammon's youngest patients are emotionally disturbed children from the Storefronts.

— Heike Gebhardt

This was the reply to the *Stern* libel:

Finest Hour of the Storefront Day Care Centers

On a Tuesday afternoon, 40 children and 30 parents from nearly every Socialist Day Care Center in West Berlin visited the publishing house of Grüner and Jahr and wrecked the spotless editorial offices of *Stern*. They went in groups to several offices and played around for about an hour. After the children got over their initial inhibitions in this antiseptic world of the *Stern* whitewash artists, they began painting the walls, knocking over wastebaskets, pounding on type-writers, trying out a fire extinguisher, practicing music — in general, by noise and movement, creating an environment that satisfied their basic needs. The *Stern* journalists, rather ill at ease, snapped photographs constantly, awkwardly offered some cookies instead of the cake they had promised, and only breathed again when the "most disobedient children in Germany" left the offices with a few pieces of booty.

*   *   *

Press Release of the Central Council of Socialist Storefront Day Care Centers of West Berlin

On Wednesday February 2, 1969, the Ninth District Court of Berlin issued a temporary injunction against the magazine *Der Stern* forbidding further distri-bution of the latest issue. The Day Care Center of Schoneberg, on the decision of the Central Council, had filed suit because *Stern* had stated in an article that parents in the centers had tried "wife swapping as an educational device." According to *Stern*, the parents had been unsuccessful in their educational work and "instead, the men began swapping wives because, according to one participant, children shouldn't be fixated on a single couple."

At the.moment, this remark is the only one being legally contested. The article contains a series of false or libelous statements, including an allegation that a three-year-old had been raped and tendentious remarks such as "Dr. Ammon's youngest patients are emotionally disturbed children from the Storefronts."

Right On! — Children and Chalk!
APO Members Demolish Stern Offices

The children's crusade marched through West Berlin's Kurfürstenstrasse. One

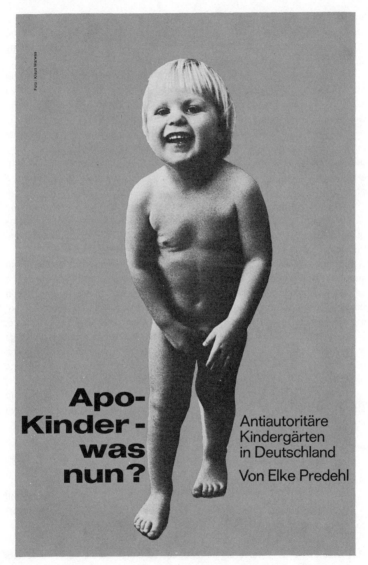

knee-high hero waved a red flag, another wore a sign on his tummy saying "My Parents are Wife Swappers — I am Liberated." What was the target of the 30 bearded daddies and furious mommies with their troop of pint-size demonstrators? The *Stern* offices in the Constanze building.

The baby-action last Tuesday was a protest against the article in *Stern* #9 on the "nonauthoritarian kindergartens," where the progeny of West Berlin leftists can run wild. For the APO, the not entirely complimentary article by Heike Gebhardt is the "fascist ranting of a liberal shithead."

In the whitewashed lobby of the *Stern* editorial offices the angry parents urged the "nonrepressed" little ones to their first revolutionary action. They ordered the diapered band to use the oil and spray paints they had brought along to spatter the walls with green, yellow, black, blue — and red, on top of that.

One father grabbed a piece of chalk to write on the wall (in black on white): "Self-criticism must happen before it's too late." Other parents tore fire extinguishers from the walls and sprayed the green display tables with white foam. Instead of painting, some of the children burst into tears out of fright.

The motley crew then swarmed into the editorial offices, where the *Stern* staff fed candy, cookies, and chocolate to the little revolutionaries. But the parents insisted on more "actions." They threw typewriters and file drawers on the floor and urged the children to rip up copies of *Stern* and documents from the archives, to break cups, mangle the potted plants, and paint the furniture.

The irritated, embarrassed children did only limited damage, but their parents made up for them: they smeared oil paints over the rugs, slashed the upholstery, tore pictures from the walls and somehow, in the crush, disappeared with one photographer's flash equipment, a table lighter, and a lamp.

At the end of the action, the educators in determined indignation tried to alter the type of "go-in" they had organized for their offspring. They took down the children's pants. But the troop couldn't perform on command.

Forty-five minutes later the parents retreated from the demolished offices. Their children were tired.

Act Three: Storefront Day Care Centers vs. the Government Bureaucracy

6 March 1969

Inquiry addressed by deputy Horst Heinschke (CDU — Christian Democrat) to the Senate on January 20:

1. Is it true that in Berlin, in so-called "Children's Communes" or "Storefront Day Care Centers," children are being educated under red banners and posters depicting Communist leaders and that the aim is: "We want our children to learn to be aggressive so that they will from an early age rise up fearlessly against the existing order," and that in Berlin the "existing order" means the

constitutional democratic government, including the Senate and the Chamber of Deputies?

2. Is it also true that the founders of these centers have applied to the Senate and the District Offices for financial support?

3. Which districts have granted these requests and which have not? How much money was given? On the basis of which guidelines or regulations?

4. Has the Senate itself allocated funds to these centers or does it intend to do so? How much money would be allocated and from what accounts would it be taken? What reasons or policies would support this decision?

5. Which churches, charitable institutions, and other organizations, definitely known to support the principles of our free and democratic constitution, have made applications for financial support in the last three years and have been refused by the Senate and the District Offices and Councils?

6. Does the Senate condone the Day Care Centers in our city which deliberately raise children to be pro-Communist and to oppose our free and democratic society?

After an interim reply, the following final report was issued on February 28, signed by the Mayor, Klaus Schutz, and by the Senator for Family, Youth, and Sport, Horst Korber:

Recent social trends clearly force on socially responsible authorities the task of initiating meaningful reforms in diverse areas of public life and responding favorably to attempts at reform made by others. The need for a policy receptive to reform is especially obvious in the educational field. To be responsive to initiatives for socio-political reform shown in the area of preschool education is, therefore, merely to be consistent.

Anyone committed to reform politics is bound to cooperate to some extent with critics of existing institutions. However, this kind of cooperation, a political necessity, can succeed only in the framework of the constitution of the Republic.

This background provides a necessary perspective to the following specific replies to your questions.

Re Question 1: The information mentioned in your question does not represent accurately the basic activities of those institutions started through parental initiative, generally known as Storefront Day Care Centers, which exemplify a specific form of preschool education. Most parents who work as teachers in these centers are guided by psychological and educational literature which has long been recognized as basic and valid.

The philosophy of the Storefront Day Care Centers can be sketched as follows:

a. education within a family-like situation as a group undertaking of several families

b. aiding the socialization process through open confrontation with authority and through the experience of solidarity and egalitarian peer group relationships.

c. cooperative work with children and group theoretical study by parents to resolve the basic questions of child raising.

It is true that some centers display the kind of décor which you mention. The Senate, however, takes the décor to be less important than the general educational philosophy; this does not mean, however, that every institution which calls itself a "Storefront Center" will be assumed to be educationally sound.

Re Question 2: Yes. Applications have been made to District Offices of the Department of Youth and Sport in Charlottenburg, Wilmersdorf, Schöneberg, Neukölln and also to the Senate Department of Family, Youth, and Sport.

Re Question 3: The District Office in Schöneberg has granted two applications and allocated sufficient funds to furnish two centers, the exact amount being 1,250 DM and, beginning Sept./Oct. 1968, additional aid for child care to the extent of 28.75 DM per day for 8 children for one center and 23.95 DM per day for 8 children for the other. This support was approved on the basis of the parents' commitment to do the supervising in the centers themselves.

It should be noted that it is cheaper for the district to provide day care in these centers than to put the children in public centers.

Re Question 4: The Senate Department for Family, Youth, and Sport, after careful consideration, has awarded money for the fiscal year 1968 from the funds marked 1000 H St. 381. The Department awarded a total of 6,800 DM to three parental groups. The use of these funds was justified on the basis of Article 8 of JWG and Article 60 of LHO to meet the minimum requirements for furnishings, toys, etc.

Second, on the basis of Article 60 of LHO, the Senate Department for Family, Youth, and Sport awarded the center at 48 Joachim-Friedrich Strasse in Berlin 1 a subsidy of 4,657.50 DM for expenses from 2.1 to 30.6.1969.

The Senate plans to continue to encourage educationally worthwhile institutions and models. As in the past, each institution will be carefully investigated before the Senate grants any financial support.

Re Question 5: To answer this question, we have made inquiries in all districts and also at the League of Welfare Organizations and the Regional Union of Youth Organizations. We conclude from their answers that:

a. No District Office of the Department of Youth and Sport and no district government has denied an application for funds in the last three years;

b. The League of Welfare Organizations and the Regional Union of Youth Organizations report that none of their requests for funds have been denied in the last three years.

An application made by the DAG-Youth Organization for funds for family vacations was filed too late for consideration in 1969, because funds for family vacations had already been distributed. But that application is under consideration for 1970.

A request from the St. John's Aid Society of the German Parish Welfare Organizations for money to build a Day Care Center was refused because the use of funds provided by the Second Special Construction Act for Day Care Centers was restricted to the needs apparent in the general labor market and the location of the St. John's Aid Society Day Care Center did not adequately meet these conditions. The Day Care Center planned by St. John's Aid Society, however, is to be included in future plans for building.

Re Question 6: No.

The Battle over the Stern Demonstration
Regional Press Association
Berlin
18 March 1969
No. 54
Inquiry in the House
Delegate Erich Mach (CDU) addressed the following questions to the Senate on March 3:

On February 26, 1969, the press reported a "go-in" of 30 parents and 40 children from the Storefront Day Care Centers at the editorial offices of the magazine *Stern* in the Kurfürstenstrasse.

I ask the Senate:

1. Is it true that the individuals involved were the supervisors at the center and children from the centers?

2. Can one view this vandalism, tolerated and encouraged by adults, as compatible with the idea of education beneficial for children (JWG Paragraph 3)?

3. Is it true that the individuals in charge of the centers urged preschool children to vandalize and soil places where adult strangers were living and working, and can this be seen as corrupting children?

4. Does the Senate still view the centers, despite these incidents, as models and as worthy of support?

The Senate's reply of March 13, signed by Kurt Neubauer, Mayor, and Horst Korber, Senator for Family, Youth, and Sport:

Re Question 1: The Senator for Family, Youth, and Sport, immediately after reading about the demonstration by parents and children in the Berlin offices of the magazine *Stern,* set in motion certain investigations of his own. These showed:

— that, presumably, the children attended some of the centers;
— that, presumably, some of the adults were the parents or one of the parents of the children in question;

— that some adults who were not members of the centers also participated. The Senate's inquiry established that the Berlin editors of *Stern* had been warned of the demonstration. They prepared for the participants by removing all important and valuable objects from the offices which were to be open and by serving a snack.

The Senate inquiry could not ascertain from which centers or other groups the participants came, because they did not give their names during the action. Upon inquiry, *Stern* said they would not bring criminal charges against the adults involved.

Re Question 2: The Senate agrees that urging and encouraging children to illegal actions, or tolerating such actions, is incompatible with education beneficial for children.

Re Question 3: When persons entrusted with the care of children urge their charges to perform unlawful acts, this endangers the welfare of the child. This is true whether or not it involves children from the Storefront Centers.

Re Question 4: The Senate asserts its interest in educational models and models of the civic functioning of the family. It will continue to be receptive to responsible citizen initiative in this regard.

The Senate is not prepared to support institutions in which children are encouraged by their parents or other adults to act in a manner which violates the most elementary rules of harmonious social intercourse.

In addition, the Senate is not prepared to encourage institutions in which parents or other adults conduct the process of education in a form damaging to the welfare of the child or — after a critical evaluation of the findings of psychology and educational science — in a form which can be predicted to damage the future welfare of the child. The Senate will support parental initiative programs and private persons conducting youth work only when the child's right to an education furthering his physical, emotional, and social competence is assured (paragraph 1 JWG).

The Senate stresses that, contrary to the misleading statements made by the press, it has never declared itself ready to support the Storefront Centers *as a group*, or to accept all the centers as models. Nor has the Senate ever said that only Storefront Centers could provide models of a family-like form of preschool education.

After investigating the twelve existing Berlin Storefront Centers, the Senate is not in a position to pass judgment on the centers as an undivided group, in terms of their educational philosophy or parental conduct. The centers differ greatly among themselves. On the basis of our present knowledge, it is clear that some lack well-founded educational ideas and that the parents, for reasons already given, have failed to offer an educational model. Therefore, the Senate does not intend to support those centers.

In other Storefront Centers no judgment can be made yet, because such experimental models need a certain period of time to produce clear results. However, at the moment no financial support is possible for those centers because the above mentioned requirement for a minimal clarity of ideas in order to measure success in achieving educational goals has not been met.

As indicated previously in our answer to Question No. 676, raised on the Senate floor, the Senate at present is supporting only one center, which will receive funds until March 31, 1969. In addition, the Office of Youth and Sport in Schöneberg supports two centers as day care institutions (cf. reply to Question 676). The Senate, in the future as in the past, will assuredly ascertain in the case of each individual center making applications, whether conditions in those centers which have been denied support have changed, and whether individual centers can be accepted as models and allocated funds.

These are the results of the libel campaign:

Regional Press Association
Berlin
32 April 1969
No. 78

Inquiry in the House
Delegate Horst Heinschke (CDU) addressed the following questions to the Senate on March 27th:

1. Is the Senate aware that a child attending a Schöneberg Day Care Center subsidized by the Senate has been brought to a physician with starvation edemas?

2. Does the Senate have an explanation for this?

3. Have any other cases of ill treatment or other deficiencies in the operation of the centers come to the attention of the Senate?

4. Does the Senate have an explanation?

5. Have these cases altered the Senate's judgment on the centers? To what extent?

The report signed by the Senator for Justice, Hans-Gunter Hoppe (signing for the Mayor), and by Horst Korber, Senator for Family, Youth, and Sport, on April 16 reads:

Re Question 1: The Senate knows of no child attending a Schöneberg center brought to a physician with starvation edemas. In addition, no child at the center has been found, on medical examination, to exhibit such edemas.

Re Question 2: In view of the above, the question is inappropriate.

Re Questions 3–5: These questions will be answered by the report which, as requested 13 March 1969, will be placed before the House of Delegates in June of this year.

Finally: The Political Results
Nothing to Complain About but the Ideology

The good will extended by the Berlin Senator for Family, Youth, and Sport towards the Day Care Centers did not prove durable. Senator Korber, who originally gave money to the centers as valuable "models of the civic functioning of the family," succinctly and unambiguously informed the Chamber of Deputies on Thursday that the Senate will not shell out any more money to the "Central Council of Nonauthoritarian Storefront Day Care Centers."

According to Korber, the Senate's justification for this step is its reluctance "to support institutions in which children are encouraged by their parents or other adults to act in a manner which violates the most elementary rules of harmonious social intercourse." In official jargon, the Senator was indicting the APO parents with the charge that education in the centers was damaging to the welfare of the children. Verbatim : "The Senate is not prepared to encourage institutions in which parents or other adults conduct the process of education in a form damaging to the welfare of the child or — after a critical evaluation of the findings of psychology and educational science — in a form which can be predicted to damage the future welfare of the child."

But the CDU, which had vigorously criticized the Senate for "over-hasty and over-generous" financial help, and which obviously thought hearty opposition to the centers was a means to get votes, could not be silenced so easily. It demanded that the Senate prepare a comprehensive report for the Youth Committee of the Chamber of Deputies.

The fact that no grounds for complaint really existed and that opposition to the centers was purely ideological was quite clear from Korber's remarks alone. Inadequacies of hygiene and absence of sanitary facilities (which, in fact, some centers had already provided) had been remedied, the Senator stated. Then he added : "These institutions are not automatically judged worthy of support even if no grounds for complaint against them exist."

— Annemarie Doherr

3. Analysis of Press and Senate Reaction to the Storefront Day Care Centers

How to Get Information

When embargoes are imposed on information (cf. Documents, pp. 94 ff.) it seems that things just begin to get interesting for the professional journalist. But there are several ways to circumvent the barrier.

One morning in a Charlottenburg center a woman arrives who says she is a secretary from Munich, explains that she is planning to move to Berlin and, not wanting to inflict the public kindergarten on her three-year-old daughter, wishes to place her in one of the centers. Her impressions of her visit can be read in the *Berlin Morgenpost* of 19 January 1969 (see Documents, pp. 95 ff.).

Two young men turn up at the Schöneberg center. They explain that they are "comrades from Munich," and that they want to start a center there; they would like to take back some informational material and photographs from Berlin. Although initially suspicious, the parents in the center that day finally agree to the request. One of the comrades from Munich turns out to be Ruitz, photographer for *Stern*.

Besides "infiltration" there is bribery, most effective with individuals who, for political reasons, reject the whole idea of our Day Care Centers (as was the case with the SEW member, J. K., cf. *Stern* 9) or with those who haven't worked very long in the centers and, prodded by some cash and friendly persuasion, will jump the information barrier. (Hence D. K., whose gullibility was ultimately used against her by the reporters, cf. *Stern* 9 — Documents, pp. 101 f.).

What to Do with It When You Have It

The division of labor in modern society contributes greatly to the "successful" style of news presentation cultivated by bourgeois editors, supposedly the guardians of "objective journalism." To produce an article in harmony with the paper's political stand, raw information is turned over to specialists for further processing. Their main job is to manufacture the general atmosphere for the article, using headlines, layout, pictures, captions, and paragraph headings. These are designed to create a particular frame of mind in the reader, and they actually have a greater impact on most people than the text itself.

Let us take two examples from those liberal magazines which always boast of their "objectivity" compared to what Springer, Inc., puts out for mass consumption.

The main photograph in the *Stern* article, also used for the cover picture (issue #9), was a composite done by Stefan Moses, who had never in his life set foot in a Day Care Center. The picture brings up all the associations which the actual text will reinforce: sexual aggression, chaos, dirt, and to top it off, a doll, symbolically brandishing its right fist, sticks out of a potty. The pictures inside, showing assorted grimy children, supplement the cover photograph and bring home the connotation that the APO (Extra-Parliamentary Opposition) is engaged in a systematic attempt to raise a generation of filthy loafers and bums, capable of nothing more than hanging around the streets and yelling political slogans they cannot comprehend.

Of course it is not accidental that the *Stern* article plays on bourgeois taboos and prejudices in condemning the new educational experiment. In a moment we shall look at the vested interests involved, but at this point it is sufficient to demonstrate how the capitalist division of labor guarantees that the data brought in by reporters will eventually fit the image set by editorial policy.

It so happens that we can show more precisely how this process works. We have the original manuscript of an article in the liberal magazine *Zeit* (24.1.1969), titled "Attempt at an Educational Model" and subtitled "Action Group in Berlin Refuses to Give Information." The original ran:

Journalists writing for the liberal press, whose audience is preconditioned to laugh, treat SDS and left wing activities as some sort of freak show. But laughter, admittedly, is permissible only if the subject can be labelled "total insanity" or an "exotic minority cult." The superficial friendliness which the non-Springer press shows towards the "serious" Left, useful if only because it permits them to launch their criticism from some half truth about the movement, vanishes promptly if class war appears even remotely possible or if the exotic threatens to disrupt the routine. . . .

The Left has discovered time and time again what happens next. In the newspaper columns the liberal values, fairness, tolerance, and free expression of opinion, turn into something else: refusal of support, authoritarianism and indignant self-righteousness. The Left knows this; the women from SDS and the Berlin Republican Club have learned from their own experience — they put an embargo on all information. The women who care about the centers, who don't just paint rooms, find and install bargain furnaces, kitchen appliances, and showers, or scrounge for funds to survive, but who care above all about working out a model of nonauthoritarian child care, need publicity to recruit supporters and help start as many centers as possible. They have found a way to avoid relying on the mass media: they will publish their own booklet (coming out next March) and make a film about their activities.

This report barely summarizes, or omits completely, our political aims. However, we don't want to criticize it, because at least the author took the embargo seriously. But we do want to show how the article looked after editorial revision.

Information is scarce and there's a reason. Says L. C., mother of a three-year-old girl and a worker in the Berlin Center, "We want to avoid having our plans written up in liberal papers as some kind of curiosity, which is what seems to have happened to Commune 1." She is a member of the Central Council, which has decided to give no information to the press and to refuse to admit observers. When the journalists inquire, as they now do nearly every week, the socialist women always have the same answer: they will publish their own information. In a booklet, which will appear in March, they will describe their institution and they will also make a film of their activities. They are interested in getting publicity — but they don't want to appear as a "curiosity."

The reader is meant to feel that the revolutionary mothers want to step right into the show window; they want publicity only at the right time, so they refuse to talk now; and they don't want to depend on liberals. Factual information — the entire point of the original manuscript, which makes it clear that factual information is not a commodity provided by the bourgeois liberal press — is, in the reworked article, "publicity" which the women desire. The final sentence is utterly cynical: "Meanwhile, they hope their Berlin bank account will grow — with the support of liberals, among others."

They generously furnish our account number at the end of the article; is it any wonder that not one liberal feels compelled to send money? (Our account number today is 7758, if any liberal feels like helping us after reading this book.)

The real reason for the embargo — our critical view of the bourgeois mass media — is simply omitted. Our criticism, verified particularly by the case of Commune 1, has been reduced in the final article to a statement that the press has made our institutions appear as "curiosities," which ignores our formulation of the *methods* used by the bourgeois press in castrating and smearing our politically relevant work and in obscuring the critical content of our institutions behind voyeuristic sensationalism.

How Exactly Does Manipulation Appear in Articles?

The *Stern* article is especially suited for studying the manipulation of fact and opinion. Let us look at page 44 of *Stern* 9 (1969), where the theoretical basis of nonrepressive education is described.

Incorrect information: " . . . the furnace stops when it drops below freezing outside. Almost all the children have coughs. In the kitchen, there are stacks of dirty dishes, garbage, and soiled diapers." Certainly the center is colder and dirtier than the public kindergarten; the reasons are obvious. But the pictures taken in the Neukölln center during the reporter's visit neither show children freezing nor suggest outrageous filth. But the reader gets the impression that the children are taken to the center deliberately to make them ill. Thanks to these absurd charges — refuted by the photographs themselves — the educational program outlined earlier literally sinks into the muck with the insinuation: "The Day Care Center is a big pile of shit."

Incomplete information: The article links the theoretical basis of nonauthoritarian education to two representatives, Vera Schmidt and Tausch. But the explanation of their work is so appallingly inadequate that there can be no possibility of even provoking serious doubts about the traditional forms of child raising, let alone explaining the reasons for nonauthoritarian education. Vera Schmidt's experiment, which was based on comprehensive research, is reduced to three bits of data: "The Russian revolution and its consequences"; "A child care laboratory founded in 1921" (just one!); "Child raising to be nonauthoritarian and without sexual taboos." Child raising without sexual taboos is the only fact that can have a concrete meaning for the reader; but again, prejudices are aroused, not calmed, because the article still, fifty years after Freud, assumes that childhood sexuality is something dirty and perverted. The two other facts are sure to exploit the anti-Communist emotionalism of the cold war: the consequences of the Russian Revolution — Stalinism — "child care laboratory" — children used as guinea pigs. All this suggests a precedent for the centers which can only arouse the reader's hate.

The article devotes more space to the investigations of the psychologist Tausch, but the seeming objectivity of that section is invalidated by the subsequent description of the "difficulties" the centers encounter, and by the remark, "Words like these, according to the believers in nonauthoritarian education, 'create the ass-kissers of the future.' " To begin with, it's not the words but the attitudes behind them and the use of prohibitions and punishments that mold the authoritarian character. Furthermore, this is not the opinion of nonauthoritarian educators alone, but of psychoanalysts and sociologists in general. The juxtaposition of our criticism of existing child raising customs with an exposition of the difficulties of the nonauthoritarian experiment superbly illustrates another technique of manipulation.

Omission of important information: No honest discussion of the problems such an experiment encounters can ignore the material difficulties involved in setting up an unsubsidized child care center. This would raise fascinating questions about why public authorities refuse to fund such nonauthoritarian forms of education. Perhaps they haven't an inkling of the harm done by traditional child raising methods and are absolutely unaware that psychoanalysts urgently call for some alternate approach? Without a thorough understanding of the criticism of traditional child raising one cannot appreciate the nonauthoritarian attempt. This slander of the centers shows precisely how far liberals will extend their tolerance: if the critics of the system actually try to implement their ideas, they don't get support, but harsh criticism, harsher than that levelled at traditional child raising. Articles such as this soon taught the Left that liberal criticism adds up to no more than support for the status quo.

Ridicule: This caption under a picture of the "good" teacher makes the concept of nonauthoritarian child raising seem ludicrous — "J. K. takes good care of his daughter Anna and all the other children in the Neukölln center. He lets them do what they want and they raise hell." Since the whole article is written in this ironic and spiteful tone, one can find many examples of the same caliber. For instance, in the collage used for the cover picture a doll, waving its right fist, sticks out of a potty. Negative associations are used to belittle child raising experiments:

In Neukölln, in the basement of a shabby apartment house in the working class district near Rollberg, the furnace stops when it drops below freezing outside. Almost all the children have coughs. In the kitchen, there are stacks of dirty dishes, garbage, and soiled diapers. The feeling of life on a barge. Capitalistic figures like Mr. Clean are locked out of the Neukölln Day Care Center.

J. K. sees signs of progress, however. "We do not stop our children masturbating and we let them play sex games in peace."

The leap from the barge-like atmosphere to sex guarantees that the reader will connect masturbation and open sexuality with filth and neglect. The description thus engenders in the reader the same feelings which he daily tries to repress and by no means helps him to overcome his ignorance about them. Invoking a masturbation/filth association only increases the need for repression. This is certainly not the way to help the reader surmount his disturbing guilt feelings; instead, it mobilizes his defenses against them.

Pseudo-objectivity: The authors, having mentioned Vera Schmidt's and Tausch's research, act as though they had done justice to the scientific reasons for nonauthoritarian education. The conclusion of the article, when Stern styles itself as the neutral observer in the battle between the Senate and the Day Care Centers, crowns this hypocrisy: "The Senate thus wishes to study the type of child raising done by those whom it habitually drives off the streets with riot sticks. These who habitually get beaten up want financial support for their child raising programs from the same people they usually demonstrate against."

What prejudices do these articles exploit?

The *Stern* article exemplifies the methods of the bourgeois-liberal press in its technique of giving vivid descriptions of matters that will mobilize defenses against anal drives in the majority of their audience: from dirty children, to the filthy building, to playing with feces and the fact that teachers frequently use words like "shit" or "crap." However, the article does not mention:

a) The reasons for a nonauthoritarian education concerning anal functions.

b) The compulsive, overanxious attitude towards dirt which pervades our society. People insist on cleanliness in the name of modern medicine, ignoring the fact that some eminent doctors think that a normal amount of dirt increases the body's resistance to disease and that sheltering in an antiseptic environment only increases the child's susceptibility to infection.

c) The damage done when anal drives are repressed and absorbed into the character structure.

d) The societal reasons for the overemphasis on hygiene in child raising.

Stern does not credit infantile sexuality with any psychological importance, as even the popular magazines sometimes do, but portrays it as dirty (see above), brutal ("he injured her during their sex play"), and harmful ("they'll all end up on the psychiatrist's couch").

The nonauthoritarian educational program, according to *Stern*, has three additional elements: aggression and neglect, disobedience, and political indoctrination. The author, Gebhard, has no trouble making these appear as dangerous and immoral tendencies. Over and over again, aggressive disobedience is described as something naturally disgusting. ("Everything got out of hand at the Schöneberg center.") Political education is meant to make Communist guerillas out of the children (they play Viet Cong). The entire article is a confused scare story of dirt, sexual perversion, brutality, and political drill, salvageable only through psychiatric intervention.

Springer, Inc. — the Berlin Morgenpost *article called, "In the Storefront Centers, Mao Ousts Little Red Ridinghood."*

This article neither emphasizes the theme of brutal and idiotic child management nor makes insinuations about the impracticability of this kind of education; instead, the description tells us that we are dealing with a very dangerous thing — a school of revolution. This is a different sort of distortion and it has a different goal. Not a word is said about sex. The article stresses "aggression" and "hellraising" and "little children busily smashing with hammers whatever strikes their fancy," and summarizes the practical aim of the whole experiment as "education for aggression."

Another difference is obvious. Stern suggests a general atmosphere of unholy mess, which can only be cleaned up by a psychiatrist. The Morgenpost's attitude, of course, is also negative and they thoroughly obfuscate the facts of our educational program. However, they see our activities as "unusual" rather than "chaotic." The new system is "astonishing" but, in its own way, it succeeds. It turns out that the "parents don't worry" (title for one section of the article) but are steadfast in pursuit of specific goals. And this is what they're after: "We want our children to learn to be aggressive so that they will from an early age rise up fearlessly against the existing order." And they are right not to "worry," because "in under one year, over a hundred centers have appeared in West Berlin." (Six in reality.)

It is also stressed that, apart from their political aims, these experiments are out of reach of those in the social class of the Morgenpost's audience. The article reports the intensive involvement required of parents — an average of two parents in the center daily, participation in frequent evening discussions, the complete subordination of individuals to the "collective" (the following sentence makes it clear what the reader is meant to think: "Anyone who won't bow to the group gets thrown out.") and the centers' "chronic poverty." In a later series on sex and the APO the Berlin Morgenpost stressed the self-defeating effects of revolutionary discipline even more emphatically:

The Commune was finished before it had even started. If at first there was a friendly echo from the bourgeois world, it was only that the bored bourgeois were dreaming of unbounded and uninhibited sexual pleasure and welcomed "promiscuity" as a diversion to brighten their existence.

— Berlin Morgenpost, 29.6.1969

A comparison of the Stern and Morgenpost articles makes it easy to distinguish the liberal and the conservative bourgeois press in regard to their opinion of nonauthoritarian education. The first

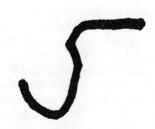

maligns it as anarchistic chaos, a case for psychiatric treatment; the latter sees it as the work of an already hated "radical minority" of students, once again on the warpath, seeking to overthrow the order which working people of our society have built. According to the conservative papers, the most alarming thing about this educational experiment is that the officials responsible for the order and security of the country don't seem to realize what's happening:

"Against the Senate"

In Berlin the children's aggression will ultimately be directed against the Senate; "We must set a good example for our children," these parents say! And the Senate is considering giving money to these people!

For the liberal middle class, the centers' method of non-authoritarian education threatens the repression to which they have grown accustomed, the rigid superego they have built. For the working class, this kind of child raising becomes "dangerous" only if political authorities fail to do their job. Both papers, as soon as we pierce the surface ideology, reveal their class character.

Manipulation in the Service of Capital

Our investigations of the Springer papers led us to the same conclusions reached in an earlier analysis, *Downfall of the Illustrated Papers*. We cite a chapter from that work: "Springer and the Students."

Springer pretended that the students' main concern was the whole issue of power. The outcome, for those who read his papers, was necessarily a feeling of disappointment at the students' brief and feeble gesture of rebellion. Workers beat up the students because their suppressed fury as victims of the system only doubled when the students failed to produce any real changes. The fury was physically brought home to the students, but they still didn't clearly understand the reason. The students attacked Springer, Inc. for its lies, not realizing that the power of the illustrated papers had its true source not in lies and distortions, but in disappointment and frustration. And it was easy to make the students themselves responsible for the workers' frustrations.

The mood of disappointment which the illustrated papers created around the student actions easily became proletarian resentment against those privileged young people who could afford gestures of protest. Because the students failed those who had believed their promise — or rather, the promise the papers made for them — to create anarchy and terror, they were perceived as part of the ruling class. Their actions were now interpreted as maneuvers by ruling class elements and taken to be insincere, because the students would soon join the power elite. . . . Disappointment over the radical change promised and withheld, attraction to the students' challenge of the powerful, bitter resignation at having been duped once again by the bosses — all these were responses which the illustrated press provoked and manipulated. Thus the populace could be turned against the students' attempts at political organization, turned against the students themselves; and so the papers could urge the oppressed to fight the oppressed (pp. 116 f.).

The Downfall of the Illustrated Papers details the methods of manipulative journalism and examines the psychological functions the popular newspaper performs for its readers. The first technique used by such papers is to conjure up an image of rampant chaos, an image generated by the sheer bulk of the kind of news they report. Murder, crime, accidents, wars, sensational events are piled up, create the impression of confusion and noise sure to profoundly shake the reader's security. At the same time, the aggressive editorial position which these papers take on every issue makes them appear a force for order. The reader, helpless in the paper's grasp, identifies with the overwhelming power of the aggressor, which seemingly controls the political life of Germany (on one occasion, even forcing the parliament to reconvene during vacation).

In regard to sex, the reader's longings are focussed on the unreachable, so that he has no choice but to accept everyday reality as it is. For instance, a picture of Brigitte Bardot, looking aggressively sexual, appears with the caption, "Be nice to your wife!" The number of sex crimes, according to the incorrect information *Bild* gives its readers, is perpetually soaring to infinity. Deluged with such data, the reader must reject his own sexual desires as some sort of monstrous alien force; the ever increasing threat of sex crimes and the constant hunt for the sex criminal force the reader to crush his desires. The papers must, however, channel this permanent state of frustration to political and social uses. At this point in the argument, we must reestimate the meaning of manipulation. The press does not seize the brains

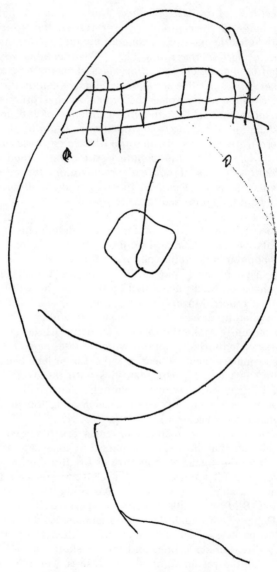

of men and make them bob up and down like marionettes. The oppression of the masses can no longer be achieved without their consent. "The Springer press presents a single option to avoid drowning in violence and oppression; one must declare one's hearty agreement with violence and oppression" (op. cit., p. 66).

Analysis of the Springer Press confirms what we have noted in the press reports concerning the Day Care Centers: it would be pointless to condemn the lack of objectivity of one particular journalist or paper, for what really matters is to ascertain whose interest is served by the mediation of information and its interpretation. Since the time that the publisher, financially responsible for the enterprise, has become separated from his paid writers, or at least since commercial acquisition of papers has become commonplace, the definition of a newspaper as "an enterprise whose salable product is advertising space, space that can be distributed through the edited parts of the paper" (Bucher) is perfectly correct. As big corporations gain increasing control of capital, the bourgeois press becomes ever more dependent on their interests, for their advertising practically finances the newspaper. We can say, with Heymann: "In monopoly capitalism, freedom of the press means that the rulers are free to tell their opinion to the workers. Springer's press, in the name of the working masses, speaks in the service of the ruling class."

— *Capitalism and Freedom of the Press*, Frankfurt, 1969, p. 158

Springer himself says the same thing in his statement of Feb. 8, 1970:

Our independence is our greatest asset. Our company upholds four principles . . .

— peaceful reunification in freedom;
— reconciliation of Germans and Jews;
— opposition to the totalitarianism of both Right and Left;
— maintenance of the principle of the socially responsible free economy.

It seems safe to assume that "socially responsible free economy" means support of private enterprise with its tendency to form monopolies and belief in a degree of state regulation. From this basic allegiance, the principles of "opposition to the totalitarianism of Right and Left" and "reunification in freedom" take their meaning. The battle with "totalitarianism" of the left is waged by this press in support of the present government, which still provides the best protection for monopoly capitalism.

All the press reports of 1969 treated the Day Care Centers as an attack on the government of West Berlin and condemned them as such. This was especially true of the *Berlin Morgenpost,* which warned the members of the Senate about supporting their future assassins.

The Senate's Position on the Day Care Centers

The Senate took a contradictory line toward the Day Care Centers. At first, it hailed the centers as "a model of the civic functioning of the family" — parents taking public responsibility — and promised financial support (cf. the letter of one Senator, pp. 93 f.). Finally, after giving several contradictory explanations, the Senate withdrew its pledge. However, local authorities did assist two centers.

Political Role of the West Berlin Senate

Despite the slogans constantly drummed into Berliners during the Cold War, the role of West Berlin is not to defend itself as a free city and to serve as an outpost of the free world against the forces of inhuman communism. In actuality, this city depends on the economic and political interests of the imperialist powers — on the same interests which produced the unification of the Western zones, external financial aid (the Marshall plan), the founding of the German Federal Republic, and finally, the rearmament of the state and its entrance into NATO.

Since 1948 the political task of West Berlin has been defined by the city's economic, geographic and political position as an island in the midst of the socialist DDR. The first mayor of the "free" sector of the "German capital" explained the situation very clearly. He wanted to use West Berlin to push for Germany's reunification as a Western capitalist state; the German "East" was an important region for its raw materials, fertile agricultural land and highly developed industries.

"Germany's destiny can be fulfilled only if we concentrate the total force of our political and economic power on the East, if," as Reuter said at the end of August, 1949, "we take the task of winning back the East as our true goal in this period of transition. The Russian paradise," he used to say, "will be unable to withstand the flood of social progress. The pressure, exerted especially by Berlin, will eventually make the Russian bear admit

that he just can't digest East Berlin! We are like dynamite in our impact on the Eastern Sector and we will be able to increase the pressure to an extent that few can as yet imagine. . . . There could be no more powerful an atom bomb for peace than developing the city of Berlin. Russia will spit out that zone like a bitter lemon.''

— W. Brandt and R. Lowenthal, *Ernst Reuter: A Life for Freedom*, Munich, 1957, p. 540, 609

Until the border between East and West Berlin was closed, the policy of making the city a thorn in the side of the DDR (German Democratic Republic — East Germany) and a show window for the West was extremely successful, due to two major causes. First, the West German economy was supplemented, especially in critical sectors, by the gratuitous addition to the West Berlin labor pool of skilled workers drained from the DDR. This bolstered the consumer prestige of the show window. The importance of this labor reservoir in the period of West German reconstruction is a well-known fact. Second, the continuing latent conflict could be used to mobilize public energies against the Communist enemy to the East. Having an opposing force against which the country could be united proved to be most convenient to the government in establishing its stability during the phase of social and political restoration. To the government of West Germany, it was well worth the regular emergency expenditures and special taxes spent on Berlin.

But after 1961 the political role assumed by West Berlin began to conflict more and more with economic common sense. For it became clear that the consolidated state to the East, the DDR, could no longer be appropriated for the purposes of capitalism without using force. However, the policy of peaceful coexistence which had emerged in 1958 made such a war almost impossible. Geographically an island with a limited labor pool, an unfortunate population structure, and uncertain access to suppliers and markets, Berlin could hardly attract larger public financial support; and to private capitalists West Berlin, under conditions of permanent cold war, seemed a rather unpredictable investment. Berlin's industry, moreover, because of the city's four-power status, could not, except where illegal maneuvers and bribery smoothed the way, take part in the rearmament boom of the rest of the country.

In order to maintain Berlin as a populated city and an attractive show window, the state was forced to pay out regular subsidies to the city, which was perpetually in a state of need. It is clear that these economically unjustifiable subsidies were designed for the advantage of private entrepreneurs, while the city population itself bore some of the cost and noncommercial sectors of the city's economy suffered. In Berlin, there are enormous problems involved in performing the role of mediator assigned to the governmental offices, for the sharp conflict between the short term interests of capital and the long term interests of society is particularly clear in this city.

It is very difficult to imagine the size and importance of the subsidies entrepreneurs in Berlin have received. In 1967 the total income tax revenue lost because of special tax exemptions given to Berlin businesses amounted to 1,848,000,000 DM, of which Berlin itself paid 668,000,000 DM. In 1964 entrepreneurs in Berlin ran up 552 million in subsidies, while the outlay for education and research was 494 million (that figure includes all schools, technical schools, universities, remedial schools, research institutes, etc.).

In 1965 the tax privileges given by the Senate to entrepreneurs totalled 590,000,000 DM. At this time, Berlin paid 620,000,000 DM in rent. In 1966 the revenue from wage and income tax in Berlin was 699 million, while the entrepreneurs received subsidies of 634 million.

We have stressed earlier that during the same period far too little was being done for public education and child care. In 1967 the Senate allocated 188,580 DM (not including building expenses) for public preschool education (18,590 places). The parents themselves paid 8,441,000 DM.

What effect did these absurd policies have on preschool education? In the spring of 1968, the deplorable situation provoked a press campaign, in which almost all the papers joined, against the Senate (cf. the first part of the documents pertaining to this chapter). The overcrowded and poorly run kindergartens could cope with only a fraction (¼) of the children who needed care. The main reason for the massive campaign against these poor conditions, however, was the acute shortage of cheap labor. Most papers, in fact, stressed the connection.

Later that year, in August, the labor shortage gave rise to proposals for kindergartens attached to the factories, as reported by the *Berlin Morgenpost* (4.4.1968). So far, however, only twelve such kindergartens, with a total of 800 places, are in operation —

and two are connected with very large businesses. It is also known that the unions oppose factory kindergartens on the grounds that they bind the worker too much to the business. This has not led the unions to conclude that if they undertook to run the nurseries, the employer could no longer use them as a tool; and the unions have not considered the possibility of making a group of employers pay for a large Day Care Center in a given area.

Why?

Basically, capitalism has an interest in factory nurseries. They free women for work. They also give capitalists the advantage of attracting female labor in a tight market. In addition, the capitalist can also directly influence child raising. For him the nursery is no social service: it is a way of securing labor. At present, however, there is such a large reserve of women and foreign workers that the companies don't really need to start any nurseries. Last, there is a factor which West Berlin's particular situation intensifies: capitalists find it advantageous to have the state provide all social services. Thus, since the worker himself ultimately pays for the services through taxes, they can reduce real wages.

So the responsibility for the miserable state of affairs in preschool education was passed on to the Senate. The press used the Senate, not the capitalists, as the target of their campaign. However, the Senate was unable, for the foreseeable future, to guarantee any fundamental changes. The Senate approved the Storefront Centers in the fall of 1968, for under the circumstances, they seemed useful: the centers were much cheaper than building and maintaining new public centers, and they seemed a way to alleviate the need for qualified preschool teachers.

Horst Korber, Senator in charge of Family, Youth, and Sport, spoke in his letter of 29.11.68 of "a model of the civic functioning of the family" and offered financial support. This remark must be understood as an offer of financial support to "parental initiative" in order to furnish an alibi for the government when the public charged them with the failure of their social policies. The Senate probably hoped that this educational model would be made available to the general public and thought this a way to fill gaps in the educational system and the labor market without spending any money.

On these assumptions, the Senate spent two months negotiating with the Central Council of our Day Care Centers. During this period, it gradually dawned on the Senate that the militants in our movement were not trying, through educational work, to create a model of the family's civic usefulness. They realized that, instead, we saw ourselves as part of the socialist movement, that we were not supporting the nuclear family as a "basic unit of the state," but attacking it as the creator of an ideology for capitalism, and that we did not see the centers as supplements to public preschool education but as a political alternative.

This growing awareness of the Senate manifested itself in the negotiations over 80,000 DM. The Senate was willing to give the money to the Day Care Centers which it chose. The Central Council saw this demand as a tactic to divide the liberal centers from the politically radical ones and, ultimately, to control and influence them through state health regulations and foster home codes. The Council, therefore, insisted that it decide which groups should receive money, and also that it control the kind of assistance given. After months of quibbling, the support failed to materialize because of those demands. No official explanation was ever given to any center.

The Senate's own public statements made clear the political motivation for its change of face (cf. LPD, Report to the Administration). By this time, the press had stopped attacking the Senate for the terrible conditions in the public day care centers and was attacking them for considering support for our Centers (cf. *Berlin Morgenpost*, 19.1.1969). The CDU (Christian Democratic Union) opposition tried to use the Senate support as an election weapon against the SPD (German Socialist Party) (major question put in the Senate by the CDU faction). There was also a growing awareness that the type of education given in the centers would never be extended to large sectors of the population. However, this awareness was not a result of considering material circumstances — lack of time, energy, and training (as the *Morgenpost* had done, see above) — but was, rather, a purely ideological matter. We read in the Senate Report of 28.6.69:

It is unlikely that the "Storefront Centers" will be the type of model for parental self-help which can be of future significance and wide application. The Senate will neither support nor accept as models "Storefront Centers" that are practicable for only a minority composed of students and intellectuals. This is especially true when they are based on the idea that education can be revolutionized only along with society itself. The Senate takes a serious interest in educational models and models of the family as a civic unit. It is receptive to suggestions made on responsible individual initiative and based on rational plans for the reform of education. The creation of homogenous groups prepared to confront and solve common problems is worth encouraging. In the education of children it is essential that such groups involve parents in the process of education.

Documents C

THE SENATE REPORT ON THE STOREFRONT DAY CARE CENTERS

Nr. 104 —
Re: the "Storefront Day Care Centers"
Document No. 666

We request that it be noted that the Chamber of Deputies in the session of March 13, 1969, passed the following resolution:

The Senate is requested to prepare a report on the private child care institutions known as 'Storefront Day Care Centers' and to give particular attention to:

The number, capacity, material assets, personnel, fulfillment of legal requirements and operating cost as compared to similar private institutions, the amount of financial support given and the results achieved, especially in regard to fundamental educational ideas and results achieved.

The following report implements the resolution.

General Background

In the course of recent years more and more young parents have attempted to work together in cooperatives to create their own kindergarten-like arrangements and to maintain them by self-help methods. The reasons for this trend are:

1. A lack of space in existing public and private Day Care Centers for three to five year-olds in particular. Because official policy considers it of prime importance that the needs of the labor market be met in order to assure the economic stability of Berlin, the children of mothers who do not work usually cannot find a place in existing Day Care Centers.

2. The general belief that kindergarten education is extremely important in childhood development and that the system of preschool education needs to be reviewed and improved.

3. The fact that many parents believe themselves to be inexpert regarding the techniques and requirements for properly raising small children and believe

that centers will enable them to provide a better environment and to learn more about children.

4. The need to combat the isolation of young urban families.

The Storefront Day Care Centers, which started in West Berlin last year, are a form of parental self-help efforts. They received their name because the first centers began operating in empty stores.

Organization, Number, and Capacity

The first Storefront Day Care Centers started in May 1968 on the initiative of different groups of parents in Neukölln and Schöneberg. In the course of 1968, two more centers were organized in Charlottenburg and Steglitz. At present the Senate knows of ten such centers, namely:

Schöneberg

Three centers, two of which have eight children apiece and are recognized as Day Care Centers and supported by the District Office; the other is just in the process of development. Eventually 24 children are to be cared for; however, very few children are now attending this center.

Charlottenburg

One center with 15 children.

Wilmersdorff

Two centers, one with 15 children and a playground directly outside, considered a kindergarten by the Senate. The other has fewer than nine children, is not considered a Day Care Center by the District Office of Wilmersdorf, and receives no support; parents and children live in the Schöneberg district.

Tiergarten

One center, found on inspection to have fewer than eight children.

Neukölln

One center with fewer than nine children; the District does not recognize it as a Day Care Center and does not support it. The parent group is looking for new quarters because the store is in an urban renewal area and is soon to be torn down.

Steglitz

Two centers, to which the District Office refused support. Not considered to be Day Care Centers. Inspection visits have shown no more than eight children in attendance.

The responsibility for each "center" clearly falls on the individual group of parents.

The parents concern themselves with all educational, administrative, and financial problems which arise in their center.

These institutions are generally open Monday through Saturday; but they close when the children are taken out on walks or excursions, swimming, or on visits and tours.

Political Background

The "centers" united in a "Central Council of Socialist Day Care Centers." Although the Central Council sees itself as a working organization in which representatives from various centers can exchange experiences on a broad basis and develop new ideas about education, the Council also sees itself and the "centers" as elements of the left wing and as part of a political movement.

This necessarily leads to conflict and tension, which occur both in the Central Council and in the individual centers. Members hold extremely diverse views. Recently, the relationship between individual centers and the Central Council has become looser. The center of action in the Council itself lies in various study groups concerned with theoretical research.

Regardless of preconceptions about one educational theory and about the political tendencies mentioned above, there is no denying that parents untrained in psychology and education are honestly struggling to learn. It would be premature to try to find a clear, general, and comprehensive education philosophy. Discussions are still in progress and issues always flare up again. It is especially important to take this into consideration since it makes it clear why the Senate has subsidized some of these institutions — as will be explained in more detail later.

Material Assets

All the "centers" started from the same negative point, in the sense that, for lack of other large available spaces, they rented stores or store rooms not especially suitable for kindergartens in terms of spatial arrangement, furnishings, sanitary facilities, and heating. Most of the stores were rather dilapidated, so that the parents themselves did the work of renovation and used their own meager resources to pay the costs.

The furnishings are shabby, usually second hand, and frequently unsuitable for children. There is a lack of suitable play material. In terms of material equipment, the "centers" hardly differ from other parental self-help organizations.

Personnel

The centers recognized as kindergartens and supported by the state, including the center in Charlottenburg, each have a trained, state-certified kindergarten teacher, hired by the parents as a supervisor. These teachers have met the legal requirements for health examinations and reports. In each of the two centers officially recognized as Day Care Centers, a mother from the parent group has assumed the duties of supervision.

In these four centers parents, either on an irregular basis or according to a system of agreements, help take care of the children and relieve the persons in charge, especially when the centers open and close each day.

In the other centers individual members of the parent group — usually on a half-day basis — take care of the children according to a systematic schedule of rotation. All parents are on duty once or twice a week for half a day.

Financial Resources

Founding and operating a "Storefront Center" is quite expensive. The costs have been borne by the parents. There are no patrons in the background, no supplementary funds. A large number of the mothers are students, being trained for some kind of profession, or working. Their incomes vary considerably. Long range operation of these institutions seems impossible without some kind of outside financial help.

For this reason most of the parent groups have filed applications with the local Youth office and with the Senator for Family, Youth, and Sport for help in founding and operating their centers.

Funds for assistance to parental self-help groups are, at present, unavailable to the administration. Help is possible only when the institution can be considered a day care center or a kindergarten.

In the fiscal year 1968, the Senate Department of Family, Youth, and Sport awarded money (from the 1000 HSt. 381 fund), the amount totalling 6,800 DM, to three parent groups in the Schöneberg area, on the basis of Par. 8 JWG and Par. 60 LHO as an emergency grant for furniture and play materials. These institutions were organized in the form of Day Care Centers and were viewed as approaches to a model of the family in a teaching function.

In the two institutions recognized as Day Care Centers the mothers in charge receive a daily payment for day care from the local Youth office, which consists of the difference between the amount prescribed by the administration for day care (6 DM per child at this time) and the amount paid by the parents. The amount paid by the parents is calculated according to the guidelines for Day Care Centers in West Berlin (Dbl. IV/1963 Nr. 54). The parents pay their share directly to the persons in charge. In addition, the Youth office has given each Day Care Center a supplementary sum for furnishings, in one case 500 DM and in the other 750 DM.

The institution recognized as a kindergarten in Wilmersdorf has received, in accordance with Par. 60 LHO and the application made by the parents, 2.30 DM per child per day (totalling 2,357.50 DM) for the first quarter of 1969. However, no additional payments have been made since that period because a report on the use of funds, required by government regulations, has not yet been received for the first quarter.

This support seems to be justifiable. After the group of parents had satisfied the legal requirements for a child care institution and had been recognized as a kindergarten, the Senate Department of Family, Youth, and Sport, after thorough investigation, subsidized the group of parents in accordance with established policy.

Legal Judgment

The "centers," like other parental self-help organizations, are difficult to classify within the existing legal framework governing children's welfare. The responsible groups do not have a corporate identity and, in fact, consist of loose alliances to achieve a specific purpose formed by parents who wish to preserve their individual self-reliance and freedom. Nor do these groups fall under the heading "Agents of Charitable Aid to Youth" (Par. 5, Sec. 4, Par. 9 JWG). The institutions claim, moreover, to provide not only care and education for preschool children (Par. 5, Sec. 1, Nr. 3 JWG) but also counselling for parents in regard to child care (Par. 5, Sec. I, Nr. 1 JWG).

The two institutions recognized as Day Care Centers and the one recognized as a kindergarten can be said, in general, to have adapted themselves to the existing legal framework. The institution in Charlottenburg is striving to be recognized as a kindergarten. As far as we know, the philosophy of the "Storefront Day Care Centers" does not prohibit adjustment to the existing categories because the style of care which the parents, or the persons they hire, give the children is the choice of the parents themselves.

Day Care Centers fall under the regulations of Sec. IV JWG (Par. 27 ff.) and Par. 36 ff. AGRJWG. Youth Offices must apply the regulations governing Children's Homes (cf. Dbl. IV/1965 Nr. 18 and 62). If the Youth Office considers care at the institution to be adequate, the person in charge is paid a daily wage (cf. Nr. 15 concerning pay for child care — Dbl. IV/1968 Nr. 46).

The centers recognized as kindergartens in Wilmersdorf and Charlottenburg, each with 15 children (the average size of groups in kindergartens) fall under the regulations for child care prescribed by the Senate in Sec. VII JWG (Par. 78, 79). The requirement that the observed inadequacies be remedied was met. The educational responsibility was assumed by a professional, who has satisfied the requirements for health examinations and for reports, as set for the good of the children. The institutions are required, according to Par. 79, Sec. 1 JWG as well as Par. 28 JWG, to request from the Senate administration permission to take the responsibility for each newly admitted child. They must meet this obligation unless notified, as is usually the case, that the requirement has been waived.

Insofar as the "Storefront Centers" have not adjusted themselves to the existing legal categories, the question of to what extent and by virtue of what regulations they come under the jurisdiction of a government youth department must be answered on an individual basis. The departments in question would be the Senator for Family, Youth, and Sport, responsible for children's homes, or the district Youth Office in charge of Day Care Centers.

Senatorial jurisdiction over children's homes applies to children's homes and "other institutions" in which minors are cared for on a regular basis, permanently or temporarily, for all or part of the day. Such a type of regular care for children during weekdays is, in fact, being provided. Thus the possibility exists of applying the regulations governing children's homes; but it must be noted that the concept of "other institutions" (Par. 78 JWG) has many possible implications which have not yet been fully explored. This is particularly true in regard to its applicability to new kinds of institutions. The case must concern an institution which, as determined by a government youth department, is in the interest of the youth in question or at least is appropriate and useful. "Storefront Centers" are institutions which, in terms of their use of space, staff, work schedules, and obligations binding the participants, can be accurately described as "institutions."

The possibility of classifying the "Storefront Centers" as "children's homes" is, however, excluded when fewer than nine children attend on a daily basis. This is clear from Par. 41, Sec. 1, Part 2 AGRJWG.

In general, the regulations governing homes and day care institutions are not particularly applicable to parental self-help organizations. The Senate Department for Family, Youth, and Sport recommends that parental self-help institutions which fall under the heading of "children's homes" meet an additional set of minimum conditions, which will be listed separately.

According to Youth Office regulations, the legal requirements for recognition as a day care institution are not fulfilled when parents take care of the children on the basis of a rotation schedule, unless a single supervisor is continually present. Only if minors are continuously cared for outside the parental home, on a part or full time basis, by another family, is it legally required that permission be obtained from the Youth Office; and in that case permission must be obtained by the person providing foster care.

It is true that rented quarters other than the parental home, in which a child is cared for by his own parents no more than two or three half-days a week, can no longer be considered to be the "parental home." There is, however, as is characteristic for family day care, no person in charge at all times, no one person who takes care of all the children and is responsible for them for the entire period in which they are outside their home.

Results

The Senate cannot yet make a definitive statement on the results obtained by the centers to date, especially in regard to their educational philosophy and its effects. The Senate has not yet been able to gain comprehensive knowledge. Conversations, visits, and study of writings or interpretations have provided only a vague and partial picture. The group of parents, moreover, regards the Senate with a reserved, wait-and-see attitude.

We can at least state that as the structure of the "Storefront Centers" differs from one to another, so does the educational philosophy of the parents who take care of a total of some 90 children. Obviously, quality varies as well.

We can say that, in general, the "Storefront Centers" are still experimental and, therefore, that their practical methods and theoretical basis must be systematized before well-founded conclusions can be drawn concerning the concrete results.

It is unlikely that the "Storefront Centers" will be the type of model for parental self-help which can be of future significance and wide application.

The Senate will neither support nor accept as models "Storefront Centers" that are practicable for only a minority composed of students and intellectuals. This is especially true when they are based on the idea that education can be revolutionized only along with society itself.

The Senate takes a serious interest in educational models and models of the family as a civic unit. It is receptive to suggestions made on responsible individual initiative and based on rational plans for the reform of education. The creation of homogenous groups prepared to confront and solve common problems is worth encouraging. In the education of children, it is essential that such groups involve parents in the process of education.

By this report, we hope to have satisfied the resolution of the Chamber of Deputies of 13 March, 1969 — doc. no. 666.

— Klaus Schutz
Mayor
— Hans Korber
Senator for Family, Youth, and Sport
Berlin, 28 June 1969

OFFICIAL PUBLICATION OF THE SENATE DEPARTMENT
OF FAMILY, YOUTH, AND SPORT

I. Administrative Regulations and Announcements of the Senator for Family, Youth, and Sport.

Encouragement of Parent-Child Groups
18.12.1969

1. Parent-child groups are defined as a number of families forming an alliance in order to educate their children in groups. They are also intended to develop the educational abilities of the parents.

2. Parent-child groups should have at least eight and no more than 15 children. The children should be educated as a group.

3. It is desirable that all parents, if possible, take part in the job of education.

4. A professional educator should be employed to advise the parents and to support them in the work of education.

5. The adults in such a parent-child group should meet regularly in order to define, in conjunction with the professional educator, the basic direction of their work.

6. The parents in such a group are responsible for supervising and educating the children. The parents are responsible for the organization of the institution. The participating parents must, because the groups are not attached to an official agency of public child care and education, name one or more persons to represent the group to the Senator for Family, Youth, and Sport.

7. Parent-child groups do not fall under the classification of foster home care.

8. Parent-child groups may receive support from available government funds. However, they have neither the legal right to claim such funds nor can they win such a right by virtue of satisfying the guidelines set by this administrative directive.

9. Grants may be made for personnel, furnishings, or rent. Rent, however, can be subsidized only if the space is used for no other purpose than child care and if the full cost cannot reasonably be met by the combined resources of all the families. Support is given only on an annual basis. Support assumes a contribution from the parents themselves and is not intended to constitute a full financing of the enterprise.

10. Application, approval, and accounting procedures will follow the usual administrative regulations of Berlin. Notification of approval signifies that:
   a. The space being used by the parent-child group is suitable and adequately furnished and equipped.

   b. After an appointment for a visit has been made, representatives of the sub-
      sidizing agency are to be admitted to the institution and to the activities
      in which the children are engaged.

   c. Professional staff should participate at least once a year in an institutional
      program for continued education.

   d. Every six months, a report of expenditures is to be sent to the supporting
      agency, with a statement from each of the families verifying their
      children's participation in the group during that period.

   e. Change of purpose, change of location, or dissolution of the parent-child
      group is to be reported promptly to the Senate Department for Family,
      Youth, and Sport.

II. A commission is being named by the Senator for Family, Youth, and Sport,
in cooperation with the District Offices for Youth and Welfare, in order to study
the encouragement of parent-child groups.

4.   The Government's Attempt to Co-opt Nonauthoritarian Education

The Changing Situation in 1970

There has been a great increase in public activity relating to preschool education. In West Berlin there are about twenty Storefront Day Care Centers, as well as numerous Day Care Centers and children's homes run by various universities, hospitals, churches, Children's Protective Agencies, etc. They have all given some thought to the idea of nonauthoritarian methods and apply such an approach to some extent. The same situation exists in the larger West German cities.

Since early this year (1970) the book market has been swamped with publications on the problems of preschool and nonauthoritarian education. The Senate, too, now encourages "Parent-Child Play Groups," which first appeared in a program for "Parental Initiative" intended to supplement public child care institutions.

According to the government code on "Family Education Measures" (18/12/1969), the Storefront Day Care Centers, although not explicitly mentioned (cf. Code, paras. 1-6), fall into this category. They are mentioned, however, in an article in the April issue of *Neue Rundbrief* by G. Stange, member of the Committee on Family Politics serving the Senator for Family, Youth, and Sport. Stange found parental initiative to have been at work long before the Storefront Centers made it "visible." She mentions so-called mini-clubs, who conduct their program, "Children in the Fresh Air and Sunshine," even in the winter, and "Children's Play Groups" sponsored by several Protestant churches and children's homes. In these programs the mothers supervised the children for a set number of hours, and regular evening meetings of parents were organized. A commission consisting of five representatives from the State Youth and Welfare Bureau and five representatives from various parental initiative groups, including one from the Storefront Centers, now determines the distribution of state support (250,000 DM) for 1970.

Does the projected support for the individual centers categorized as parental initiative groups indicate a change in the Senate's attitude towards the Storefront Day Care Centers? If not, what does it mean?

Supporting Parental Initiative — An Alibi for the Senate?

In our introduction and our analysis of the press campaigns against the Senate in the spring of 1968, we analyzed the basic societal contradictions behind the miserable condition of preschool education in Berlin. The economic contradictions, of course, continue as before and still have the same effect on the educational sector. (Note the contradiction between the technical, financial, and scientific potential for a better educational system, which would be advantageous to capitalism, and the actual failure to invest in this sector, which means that Day Care Centers exist only for a fraction of the population and that repressive methods must be used in education.) When our centers opened, the press stopped all campaigns against the deplorable lack of day care facilities, and the basic problem was somewhat overshadowed when the mass media and various political factions began to redirect their attacks against the centers.

Is there any chance, in the near future, of an improvement in preschool education? Two examples will adequately answer this question. First, the Senate itself declared bankruptcy on the working class suburb of Wedding. The conclusions of its report on predicted developments to 1972 are simple: things will get a lot worse (cf. LPD 29.5.69). The protest movement of West Berlin kindergarten teachers in 1969 had equally significant results. Because of unbearable conditions in overcrowded schools, the teachers issued a set of demands, consisting of three main points:

1. Admissions must be frozen and the size of classes decreased.

2. Teachers must get on-the-job training and continued education.

3. It must be understood that the teacher's job is education, not administration.

When all sorts of democratic pressures by professionals failed to win any response from the responsible bureaucracy of the

Berlin Senate, the teachers decided on a one day warning strikᴇ The Senate, aided by political parties, press, and unions, did everything in its power to prevent this — including personal letters threatening to fire any teacher who went on strike. The pressure worked. At the last minute, the strike was called off and the teachers were consoled with the promise of discussions between their union and the Senate. None of their demands has been recognized — let alone met — as yet, but teachers' salaries have been increased slightly.

A glance at the Berlin schools shows an equally bleak prospect. The problem only attracted public attention in March 1970, after School Senator Evers retired and the students and teachers took joint action. When *Spiegel* (no. 12, 16.3.70) interviewed Evers, he explained why he could no longer work on the school emergency: "Yes, the inadequate financial plans of the Berlin Senate will effectively end school reform for several years and will even make the situation deteriorate further."

Had Evers asked for too much? Evers: "The Federal Cultural Council will soon publish an overall plan which is in agreement with my own demands. Their financial proposals will prove that my financial demands were moderate, considering the needs of our educational policy."

"Moderate," that is, in terms of the "needs" of a system of class education; it means, essentially, providing money to cover the increasing number of students and to hire teachers to remedy the chronic shortage (the plan envisions a tenth school year and, eventually, an all-day school). Evers was trying to use the model of technocratic college reform to improve our nineteenth-century class education. Let us quote him to illustrate just how obsolete, even for capitalist conditions, the German school system is:

Comparable industrialized countries allocate almost double the percentage of the gross national product — 8 percent or more, as opposed to our 5 percent — to culture and education.

However, the Federal Republic is striving to reach 8 percent by 1980.

This is 1970. Ten years from now will probably be too late. I am afraid that the German educational system has already begun to collapse.

Concretely, this is the situation: we will have one million university students by 1980, but about eleven million students in the

stem. I don't understand why only one million
optimum training. . . . If teachers' salaries continue
t the same rate, we will just be able to cover the
ost of personnel. . . . This is exactly what is so horrible
situation, that bad working conditions in the schools
iduates reluctant to become teachers.

e demands of the students, as stated by the SPD, actually go
it further than the governmental "educational policy" (cf.
udent Resolution, 10.3.70, "Agit-883" #53, 13.3.70, p.4).

RESOLUTION
UNANIMOUSLY ADOPTED BY THOUSANDS OF BERLIN STUDENTS
MEETING IN THE TECHNICAL UNIVERSITY
MARCH 10, 1970

The students who gathered March 10 in the Technical University wish to express their indignation concerning the Senate's recent attempt to let existing conditions and opportunities in education deteriorate even further. We know that the decay affects most severely the children of workers and the working class itself, which is supposed to remain inarticulate and to continue to submit to exploitation without protest. Therefore, it is clear to us that the Senate's repeal of its recent act decreasing the educational budget is not enough.

Our main demand, "Equal Education for All," leads to others. We demand that the Senate restore the 570 million DM which it cut from the educational budget, that it do so by Tuesday, March 17, and that it deduct the same amount from the police budget, in order to meet the following conditions:

1. For the students:
   — SIX-HOUR DAY AT ALL SCHOOL LEVELS
   — SUBSISTENCE PAYMENT OF 500 DM TO ALL
     STUDENTS
   — PAID VACATION AT LEAST SIX WEEKS LONG
   — BETTER EDUCATION TO SHORTEN SCHOOL YEARS

2. For the schools (particularly the main high schools where an extra year is planned):
   — ACCREDITED SCIENTIFIC AND TECHNICAL
     EDUCATION

> — INTENSIVE AND REALISTIC VOCATIONAL
> GUIDANCE IN THE TWO YEARS BEFORE
> GRADUATION
> — PAID WORK EXPERIENCE IN THE SENIOR YEAR,
> BUT NOT IN JOBS, LIKE TEACHING, WHICH
> PERPETUATE THEIR EXPLOITATION

The students here present declare that if the Senate fails to meet these demands by March 17, they will continue their open struggle against the Senate through further actions and demonstrations.

We have established the point that there will be no improvement in preschool education in West Berlin in the near future. And the prediction holds for the entire Federal Republic.

In this context, what does encouragement of parental initiative mean?

We need to look a little more closely at the official policy, as well as its official and semiofficial basis. The program for "Parent-Child Groups" has been allotted 250,000 DM for 1970. According to Stange's report, this program covers about 250 groups (47 Mini-clubs, 140 Play Groups, 20 Day Care Centers, 5 "Cooperatives"), which comes out to about 1,000 DM per group per year. It is true that by the deadline in March 1970, only about 30 groups (15 were our centers) had applied for money. Could this be because Mrs. Stange, acting in the interest of the "civic functioning of the family," named an extra 200 nonexistent groups?

But the support is' inadequate even for the 30 bona fide groups: each will get a maximum of 700 DM per month, just enough to pay the teachers and, with luck, the rent. No matter how the money is divided, it isn't enough for the existing groups. It certainly isn't enough to stimulate parental initiative. Since the budget cannot be significantly increased in the next few years, the purpose of the whole program — encouragement of parental "potential for educational work" — is feasible for only a tiny group. The guidelines of the program also eliminate certain population groups from eligibility for state aid.

Point 3 requires that all parents participate in practical educational work, Point 5 that they attend regularly scheduled meetings, Point 6 that they participate in planning the facilities, and Point 9 that the parents themselves make a proportionate financial contribution. Taken together, these conditions make it impossible for workers to reach the circle of the elect. Contrary to Mrs. Stange's claim, it is clear that so far only middle class groups — notably academics — have applied for funds.

So the loudly heralded "encouragement of parental initiative" has absolutely no effect on the miserable state of affairs in pre-school education. It is easy to see through the Senate's maneuver. In the past, the Senate has been held accountable for an intolerable situation and it will come under much harsher criticism in the future. Supported by parents interested in education, the Senate has initiated, with a conspicuous flurry of propaganda, a "modern experiment" which it can hold up before the critics.

Despite the fact that the real nature of the situation is unmistakable, the Senate's semiofficial propaganda constantly hails the parental initiative program as the cure for all our ills. We can cite two articles: "Between Home and Kindergarten" by Dr. Arno Kosmale, Director of Social Work in the Senate Bureau for Family, Youth, and Sport (he has since left to work in Bonn's Welfare and Family Department), published in the *Landespressedienst* of June 16, 1967, and G. Stange's "Encouraging Parent-Child Groups in Berlin" (cited above). They begin by acknowledging that both family and kindergarten inadequately perform their present task:

The small family, especially the young couple, lives in isolation. Marriage, especially in the first few years, means that the couple is primarily concerned with each other. . . .

Usually absolutely no preparation is given for marriage and child raising. Young parents raise their children either on the model of their own upbringing or in direct reaction against it. . . . The modern family does not give children adequate social experience . . . there is far too little contact with peers. The modern residence — separate tiny apartments in huge and densely populated districts — prevents friendships with neighbors instead of encouraging them. . . .

In summary, we can say that there is no doubt, among scholars or laymen, that the social functioning of the "average family" justifies the belief that it is structurally deficient as a child rearing institution . . . If other institutions (day care and infant care centers, kindergartens, shelters) are to compensate for this deficiency they must concentrate on the areas where the nuclear family fails. But this, it seems, is precisely what they cannot do. If we look at the actual situation in day care centers, we see:

Day care centers do not function to relieve the isolation of the young family . . . they hardly help parents to think critically about the matter of child raising, to learn the various methods, to gain confidence in their task, and to develop their capabilities. Children are given strictly professional care in these centers. They are brought there and taken home later. There is room for only 23 percent of the three- to six-year-olds. . . . The size of the class (usually 15 but sometimes more), the twelve-hour day, the job of babysitting and being on the lookout for trouble, often prevent the attainment of educational goals.

— Kosmale, *Between Home and Kindergarten*, 1969

From the dissatisfaction with family and kindergarten as child raising institutions follows a recommendation for the encouragement of "Parent-Child Play Groups" as a "supplement to family life" which would develop "parental potential for child raising." The chances for this plan, as we have already made clear, are slim or nonexistent.

Both articles reject the Storefronts' nonauthoritarian style of education:

As always with innovations, the contours and structures are not perfectly clear at the beginning. Thus the progress of certain "Storefronts" shows that propagating counter-styles and ideas that exist only in reaction to the prevailing system of thought neither provides a workable model nor helps us to pattern better child raising methods and better educational techniques. Other institutions, through practical and self-critical work, have made substantial contributions to the theoretical basis for the new "Parent-Child Play Groups."

— Kosmale, op. cit.

Of course not a scrap of evidence specifying either the failures of nonauthoritarian education or the significant contributions which other groups have supposedly made appears in support of this libel. But Mrs. Stange's criticisms are more suggestive:

These centers were conducted . . . according to a conception of "nonauthoritarian" education. However, the aim of reaching the worker and his family through such child care work was not fulfilled because the young academics, typically from middle class backgrounds, assumed in the workers a consciousness of being underprivileged which the workers did not have. The rejection of order and cleanliness as values — values which have supported

*our social order for centuries — likewise barred communication.
The workers were not enthralled by Latin expressions for simple
German ideas; they were suspicious. If one wants to reach work-
ers, one must talk to them in a language they understand.*

We don't know where Mrs. Stange got the idea that we speak
Latin to workers. Members of the centers also never made a systematic effort to propagandize workers about "nonauthoritarian
education." The reason had nothing to do with communication
difficulties; instead, we realized after an experimental period that
even assuming that nonauthoritarian education is suitable for
proletarian children, the material conditions of a worker's life
prohibit this form of parental initiative. But Mrs. Stange has a
reason for libelling the centers. She is expressing the fear that
the proletarian masses, through an awareness stimulated by education, might become conscious of contradictions which have been
cleverly and deliberately concealed from them. This could happen
if a revolutionary organization encouraged such a consciousness.
Therefore she mentions several times that a variety of population
groups have filed for support for "Parent-Child Play Groups." It
is easy to prove, however, that this claim is a lie.

It is easy to see from all this that, in a situation as economically
and politically distorted as West Berlin's, there is only one way to
get urgently needed partial reforms. The psychological insights
which underlie nonauthoritarian education must slowly filter into
the educational institutions as far as their repressive structure
permits. That is the only "success" which the glut of critical
literature can produce in the near future.

The liberal's dilemma appears most clearly in the writings of
the more progressive critics. We will use as an example an article
by Herman Minz, "New Educational Perspectives on the Kindergarten," which also appeared in the April issue of the official
publication from the office of the Senator for Family, Youth, and
Sport. Minz is a professional in the government-run Day Care
Centers, Section III.

Minz establishes that

*in the country which originated the kindergarten, preschool
education is now far behind that in many countries of Western
Europe, North America, and the Eastern Bloc. . . . Among
the first ten European countries, ranked on the percentage of
children which kindergartens can accept, the Federal Republic*

holds sixth place, after Belgium, the Netherlands, France, Italy, and Switzerland.

Minz suggests that kindergartens are ignored as a minor offshoot of education proper because:

1. *Day Care Centers and shelters have been seen primarily as a service for working mothers.*

2. *They therefore concerned themselves with "the lowest population strata — consequently, the physical facilities and furnishings, as well as the training and the professional and social status of the teachers, have been unimpressive."*

3. *Not enough recognition is accorded the unique importance of early childhood. Kindergarten teachers are still not taught psychoanalytic insights on early childhood, insights of a significance one can hardly exaggerate.*

General dissatisfaction with the educational system has, in the last few years, extended to the area of preschool education. Such spectacular experiments as the "preschool reading movement" and "nonauthoritarian Storefront Day Care Centers," which became popular topics for newspaper and television reporters, have now led even the man in the street to concern himself with such problems.

Since the "preschool reading movement" limited itself to research and ended many years ago, Minz's statement amounts to an admission that the practical and political work performed by the centers was required to produce a "change."

Minz opens the second section of his article with this sentence: "Today, the conclusions of the research on preschool education can be viewed as sufficiently firm to justify *new goals* for the kindergartens and the introduction of *new methods*, at least on an experimental basis."

Minz thinks the most important findings are:

Today's family, even when its existence is secure, cannot adequately socialize the child . . . Today, therefore, one can assume an almost unanimous consensus for demanding that institutions which supplement the family carry on part of the education of the small child.

Intellectual development depends largely on age, is half com-

pleted by age four, and depends almost totally on environmental stimulation.

In regard to children disadvantaged by an unfavorable socio-cultural milieu . . . it can be assumed as established fact that belonging to a given social level and experiencing the influences of its particular environment decisively affect an individual's total development, especially his intellectual growth (our emphasis).

These statements, coming from a member of the government, sound almost like revolution. At two points, however, in Minz's line of reasoning his bourgeois ideological bias is obvious. First, he does not examine further how a person's educational and cultural fate depends on his social "strata" — one gets the impression that the underprivileged are but one of many levels. Where he should treat the material exploitation of the proletariat as a highly relevant fact, he uses the apolitical term "unfavorable." Second, he does not analyze the relationship between education and strata, in terms of the social, ultimately economic, causes. A naive idealism thus characterizes Minz's "urgent recommendations" in the third section of the article:

1. *We require kindergartens for all children when they are three years old.*

2. *New educational methods and content: . . . we are far more concerned with the development of a general cluster of characteristics and behavior patterns which the democracy of the future will demand of its citizens. Sexual enlightenment in theory and actuality: Despite all the observations of in depth psychoanalysis, our kindergarten children are still treated as asexual creatures, which they undoubtedly are not.*

Extension and intensification of parental participation. Additional opportunities for diagnosis and treatment of children with behavior problems stemming from environment.

3. *Specialized professional consultants: psychologists, teachers with a background in psychology, speech therapists, occupational therapists.*

4. *Close cooperation with schools.*

"Even this short article clearly shows that any improvements made in preschool education will cost a great deal of money, and it would be unrealistic not to acknowledge that this is one of the major difficulties in meeting our demands." But we all know by now that the only demands which will be met in the next few years are the ones that won't cost any more money.

Therefore, the conflicts which Minz, towards the end of the article, predicts in the attempt to institute his program have already been decided. He speaks of competition with other demands — e.g., for school buildings, old age homes, hospitals, etc. He also mentions conflicts of "purpose" for kindergarten education: should there be more Day Care Centers built, of the usual type but with more generous plans for space and learning materials; or should there be an increase of personnel and more intensive care in the existing centers; or should more emphasis be placed on developing new kinds of groups? The answer is a foregone conclusion. In 1970 the Senate decided to cancel all plans to build more Day Care Centers. In view of this fact, the author's final recommendation can only be interpreted as poker-faced cynicism: "These closing words are not meant to induce resignation, but to stimulate a new commitment."

This essay well represents the character of all the progressive literature on preschool education — ample rhetoric plus criticism based on research findings. But the whole effort remains in the clutch of the ruling bourgeois ideology, responsible for transforming social conflicts into controversial issues, in order to make the solution seem to depend on accepting recent scientific information, and for ensuring that no one wonders what economic and political forces actually dictate the situation. Liberal critics also present problems separately, without making political connections; as a result, their demands either seem unconvincing or resigned to the impossibility of social change. In reality, this kind of article performs five major tasks:

1. To obscure the fact that the availability of child care and education is determined by class.

2. To deny the economic cause of contradictions in the educational sector — namely, the short-term profit drive of private enterprise.

3. To ensure that concerned individuals commit themselves to unrealistic demands (see Point 2).

4. To prepare the ground, having created an atmosphere of general resignation, for approval of partial reforms advantageous

to capitalists, not parents and children.

5. Above all, to veil the connection between the poverty in the educational sector and the contradiction basic to authoritarian capitalism; change in education, as in all other areas, presupposes the recognition of this contradiction.

Our interpretation of contradictions in the educational sector came from analysis of West Berlin's specific situation, but it applies to monopoly capitalism as a whole. As for future developments, we can predict only general tendencies. It is clear that in the long run, monopoly capitalism requires a more efficient educational system, one directly linked to the needs of the economy, which will continue to assure the domination of man by man. Hence when viewed objectively, the present protests in colleges, schools and preschools, as well as the general trend towards enlightened liberalism, will only support capitalism until the critics strive, with the masses, to transform the relationships of production.

This is true even when an individual believes, subjectively, that he is aiding the progress of humanity, but refuses, objectively, to join the struggle by working with the exploited. Technological progress requires that the expanding monopolies systematically and manipulatively extract a certain degree of team work from the workers of the future. In the long run this will affect the goals set for early education, because preschool education lays the foundations for later skills, capacities, and intelligence. (This trend is already evident in the preschool program of the Berlin John F. Kennedy School.)

The ongoing university reform functions partially to provide trained leaders for industrial concerns and bureaucracies. One can predict that the trend to reform will extend through the school system and down to the kindergartens. Already, the tendency toward state control of the educational and child care system, covering all children from the third year or even earlier, is visible. However, the inner contradictions of the capitalist system obstruct the full actualization of the government's goals.

One thing is certain: in the future, as in the present, reforms within the system cannot profoundly change material conditions in the lives of the wage earning masses.

5. Changing Policies in the Storefront Day Care Centers: Dissolution of the Central Council and the Initiation of Community Work

SDS Work Conference, April 1969

One of the nine workshops at the 1969 SDS work conference in Frankfurt concerned "Day Care." The members held many discussions to try to link a critique of previous work with new plans for a more politically oriented child raising. We will reprint the workshop's final written report, which summarized their conclusions. The paper should not be taken as a definitive program for the whole educational sector. Rather, the paper attempts to compare the actual situation in certain areas with possibilities for political change, taking into consideration the present state of the socialist movement, and to outline some conclusions. During the course of 1969, the new directions proposed at the end of the report were greatly modified, and we will discuss these changes.

From Nonauthoritarian to Socialist Education
The dissolution of the old class relationships, predicted by Marx, began during the Weimar period, which favored monopoly capitalism. After World War II, Germany's late capitalist society saw the objective proletarianization of the middle class. The once propertied and economically self-sufficient middle class became progressively more dependent; like the proletariat, it lacked its own means of production. The process of proletarianization pulled down, along with the rest of the middle class, those whose intellectual qualifications had lost their former market value; these

intellectuals were now cut off from the chance of accumulating capital. The student protest movement was the first response of German youth to this new situation. Owing to the very occurrence of a real protest, however, training of critical powers is now almost never given in the schools. Success in the existing educational system means giving masochistic consent to one's own intellectual and emotional numbing.

The situation creates increasing insecurity for those students who criticize it, for their careers are jeopardized. They find it impossible to use their middle class status as a means to any kind of search for happiness and self-fulfillment. A middle class social position now implies support for the repression of the lower classes and for the terrorism perpetrated by a ruling elite. As soon as students actually try to live in liberated ways and to press for the liberation of others, official repression of their actions becomes more severe.

Protest also endangers the future of one's own young children. The children of middle class intellectuals cannot have a satisfying future now unless the goals of the parents' political struggle directly and objectively correspond to the interests of these children and unless the children are raised by methods appropriate to let them carry on the political struggle themselves.

Despite the middle class's loss of economic autonomy, it still clings to the Humboldt ideal of educating a man to be autonomous and individualistic — an ideal that has long since lost its economic justification. Things were different at the beginning of bourgeois society. In the days of early capitalism and free competition, the bourgeois individual experienced something foreign to the peasant masses and the urban poor — he worked as an individual from his own capital. After 1848, however, the Humboldt style of humanism became associated with the militaristic, imperialistic, and authoritarian interests of the Prussian power elite; after 1871, when that elite took over in Germany, it ruled an economic capital that was becoming more and more concentrated. In the heyday of capitalism, humanism and militarism together shaped bourgeois education.

The student movement began by protesting this authoritarian reactionary education and tried, by means of nonauthoritarian educational experiments, to counter and to eliminate the oppressive influence of the bourgeois family; it did not attempt to make a simultaneous attack, logically necessary, on the foundations of oppression through the family.

Since nonauthoritarian education started by using the models of Vera Schmidt and A. S. Neill, it was in no position to prepare children for a radical stand or to teach them how to defend their interests against an authoritarian system of monopoly capitalism. A more political kind of education, one that would prepare children to fight the system, was clearly necessary. We found it easiest to formulate this endeavor as proletarian education: education which envisages its ultimate aim of multidimensional human beings as attainable only through the triumph of a movement which, by working for socioeconomic change, will be able to overthrow social tyranny and oppression.

Education for political change is necessary to give children and adults in collectives a chance to extend their own socialist effort, in order to create, ultimately, a society in which free and autonomous people can live together.

In thinking about education, we must go beyond a model of the nonrepressive family and look at the concrete requirements of the class struggle. The first step is the elimination of antiworking-class prejudice from early education. Proletarian education involves ending both sexual and political taboos in child raising. It involves giving children, as young as possible, a clear idea of the social causes of oppression. It encourages them to try, at the level of their own ability, to attack those causes. Education occurs not in the family but in the struggling collective.

The most important model of nonauthoritarian education used by the Storefronts and Collectives in operation at this time is Vera Schmidt's Moscow Child Care Laboratory. Her purpose was to prevent the pattern of instinct deformation caused by the traditional father-mother-child triangle in the bourgeois family. The experiment used a neutral educator to replace parents, who, consciously and unconsciously, act as agents of existing society by passing on societal norms which they have internalized.

This educator, by consciously maintaining an effective distance and a neutral attitude to the children's desires and play, would permit an optimum development of the child's instinctual nature.

The experiment was broken off after three years. No data exists, therefore, to verify whether this model of a comprehensive "nonauthoritarian" education, in terms of social psychology, really tended to prevent neurosis, whether it met the needs of Soviet society (which had then undertaken to build a socialist state), and whether it could, without drastic modification, be transferred to other societies.

The Child Care Laboratory in Moscow was an "educational island" far removed from the real world, for the children were not prepared for their lives in Soviet society. (Summerhill is an even more extreme example of school's insularity.) Education as practiced by Vera Schmidt prepared children to enter a society which permitted total instinct gratification, not for a society where they would have to fight for this right.

The West Berlin Storefront Centers had their roots in women's attempts at self-liberation; they wished to free themselves from the woman's traditional role in the nuclear family in order to join the political struggle. The centers, a spontaneous development, did not take their organization and educational principles from the political demands of the movement, even though they did reproduce internally the phases of antiauthoritarian revolt which occurred in SDS.

The basic tenet of education in the centers is the belief that needs should be freely satisfied in the children's collective. Instincts should no longer be repressed; they should be worked through and sublimated. Psychological energy can then be used productively because it no longer creates guilt and fear, nor must it be bound up in suppressing the instincts. The idea is to provide a basis for the development of ego-strength, in the strict psychoanalytic sense of the term, without the implication of adjustment to society.

The second principle was to develop the child's autonomy by using life within a collective to end the attachment to parents alone. If the children are less fixated on their parents and on parental behavior, their lives will not revolve around repetition compulsions generated by norms internalized through parental coercion. Success means that an authoritarian character cannot develop.

Given the new educational mechanisms in late capitalism, which strip away ever more of the family's influence on the socialization of children, education for autonomy can also mean that the children are less swayed by the pressures which social institutions exert on their lives (cf. David Riesman — "outer-directed type"). It also means that the children will learn to choose their own activities and to form groups within the limits set by the needs and interests of other children in the collective.

Our nonauthoritarian education, however, sometimes functioned on the same abstract level as the corresponding anti-authoritarian phase of SDS, as a purely negative reaction to the status quo. Children can be educated to serve the movement only by helping them acquire the ability to sublimate enough of their instincts to take part in the ongoing fight and by orienting them to the present stage of the class struggle — not by merely reproducing in them the tension in the movement between anti-authoritarian rebellion and the quest for revolutionary discipline.

How does the reality principle, the ability to work through independently and to comprehend the contradictions fundamental to existing society, actually work in a child's mind? If we can assume optimistically that "at any given moment, the reality principle is operative in the free and critical child," a liberating education is enough to produce active political resistance later.

But aren't children in a nonrepressive situation segregated from society by that very fact? Doesn't the concept of ego-strength, therefore, classically defined as the optimum equilibrium between the demands of id, environment, and superego, have to be redefined in political terms? We have to reevaluate id and environmental demands, no longer just wanting the individual to experience and recognize the outer world (social reality) as an instinct-suppressing force, but rather, wanting him to analyze that force and consciously to postpone gratification of and to sublimate his desires, in accordance with a realistic assessment of changes that must be made in the environment.

This means, first, that children must learn in the collective to disentangle and understand their own needs. The norms by which instinctual gratification is limited, moreover, must not derive from the traditional superego, created from ego fragments no longer accessible to and comprehensible for the conscious ego. The norms should be clearly communicated by the parents' political activity. They should not be internalized in a rigid form, but should be flexible enough to meet the child's changing needs. These norms should serve to guide the child without becoming internalized agents of society and tyrannizing the ego.

Although we don't have the knowledge or experience to specify concrete situations which would produce these results, we can at least name one requirement: the children must continually confront both social realities and the struggle to change them. Something like this usually happens even in merely nonauthoritarian education (outings on public transportation, in public playgrounds, and in the neighborhood). In order that the children work out the conflicts which they see on these trips, the adults must articulate them and give a political interpretation.

But interpretations could be received in a spirit of resignation or could even lead, when there is a prolonged exposure to a repressive environment which forbids pleasure (e.g., school), to nostalgia for the children's collective (in the form of intensified demands for protection), unless children are given, simultaneously, a chance to participate with their parents in real acts of resistance. Renunciation and the beginning of revolutionary discipline, then, do not remain abstract ideas.

Socialist child raising, like nonauthoritarian education, attempts to spare the child the repression of instincts characteristic of bourgeois life. Therefore, it must at first insulate a world for the children detached from both family and society. But for socialist child raising it is not enough to discover that a different environment can produce different children: the children must eventually be able to change the environment themselves to meet the needs of the people.

The children, therefore, must confront other children, outside the collective, and learn in specific instances of social conflict how to insist upon and communicate norms acquired by living in the collective. In this way, the child prepares himself for the struggle in school, for the confrontation with brainwashed students and teachers.

Socialist education must put an end to the bourgeois taboo on politicizing children. It must enable the child, by giving him both sexual and political information, to influence the "children of the masses" when he meets them in public kindergartens, in playgrounds, and in courtyards. The Day Care Center will not be an educational island, but the home base from which children, along with adults (from the parents' collective), go forth to collective, militant action. In the socialist children's collective, the child can learn to handle materials used in agitation and public information and he can, through political children's theater and games as "representations of the social struggle," absorb concepts which his ego will transform and put to further use in the later struggle for liberation.

Critique of a Purely Psychoanalytic Approach to Early Education

Practical Beginnings of Socialist Child Raising
An approach to early education concerned only with avoiding

the psychic disasters stemming from clashes with family authority has no inherent political potential.

For the centers, the value of psychoanalytic insight lies in its total belief in need gratification as the first and necessary step towards children's liberation. Part of this program is observing the symptoms of repression seen in children and trying to uncover their sources.

Since coercion by society produces repression within the family, children experience instinctual repression at one remove. The causal political situation tends to act on the child only through the family's repression of his drives. Therefore, in raising children, one must break out of the narrow family context and directly confront political reality.

Freedom to Masturbate Is Still a Bourgeois Privilege!

The antiproletarian character of nonauthoritarian education is evident in its results — freedom from repression creates a strong ego in children only to make them more vigorous members of the privileged bourgeois class.

Releasing repressed energies does not suffice to make a socialist. This kind of education is bourgeois precisely because it avoids any experience of class conflict. At present, class conflict means the unorganized revolt of the bourgeois intelligentsia; and they should not isolate their children from this experience. Confronting the political struggle, seeing the social situation, means the child is in touch with political reality. This endangers, though in a rationally manageable way, the barren, deceitful illusion of total instinctual gratification in some childhood paradise.

Parental Collective and Child Raising

It was generally agreed that some form of parental initiative should complement the children's education in the collective (due to the fact that the nuclear family tends to reproduce repressive social norms and mechanisms of coercion, the need for the child to find continuity of experience between life in the collective and at home . . . , etc.).

In reality, the parents' meetings usually degenerated into impromptu psychologizing chats or apolitical study groups, their only common interest being the children. There was a widespread notion that the organization of children's collectives constituted in itself a political act, since the original intention was to end the separation between politics and private life (cf. paper of the Women's Action Council of the DK, 1968).

However, the parental collective turned into a kind of interest clique. It is true that discussion in the collectives of children's conflicts (using the center's files) led to finding the source in marital rifts and parental emotional problems, which in turn could often be isolated and traced to certain authoritarian personality patterns, caused by societal factors and upbringing, which were duplicated in the marriage and passed on to the children. Parents recognized the impossibility of dissolving these patterns within the bounds of the family, which caused the break-up of marriages and an exodus into communes.

Unfortunately, however, when people joined communes to solve their personal problems and saw them as "pacified zones" — prefigurations of socialism rather than militant cells — the communes became ends unto themselves and sometimes even inhibited engagement in political activity.

The communes did make nonrepressive child raising easier (for one thing, there was less fixation on parents), but the ideals of resistance and struggle, unless transmitted through collective political action, remained abstract.

Parents in collectives rather than communes also found that they could not concentrate on child raising alone; they had to work on parallel political problems and undertake actions that transcended immediate parental concerns and required collective organization. IT IS IMPOSSIBLE TO POLITICIZE PARENTS THROUGH CHILD RAISING ACTIVITIES ALONE! ! !

Our work conference made three main proposals for parental collectives:

1. Separate the radical and liberal parents in centers.
2. Cooperate with workers organizations, e.g., in organizing factory kindergartens.
3. Prepare children for resistance in schools, e.g., by founding school-connected centers for after-school care.

Formation of a New Central Council

The major papers from the SDS conference were printed in Frankfurt in "Day Care Centers — INFO 7" and had important effects on the West Berlin Day Care Center movement. The first result was a political resolution:

RESOLUTION TO REESTABLISH THE CENTRAL COUNCIL OF
SOCIALIST DAY CARE CENTERS IN WEST BERLIN

The undersigned groups believe that the work done so far by
the Central Council was insufficient to identify the fundamental
problems of the West Berlin Storefront Day Care Center movement, let alone solve them. We believe that further work in a
Central Council must produce a critical analysis of the progress
of the movement, leading to resolutions that can be applied
in action.

We know from experience that although this society might
support nonauthoritarian education, it will certainly never help
socialist child raising intended to generate militant cells for the
struggle against the present system. We must realize that no
existing institution can be turned to our use. The (financial)
tactics of the Senate were designed to fragment the Central
Council, to make certain centers economically dependent and
ideologically weak. The only proposal we could accept, financial
support for the Central Council itself, was never even a possibility
for the Senate.

The undersigned centers, therefore, feel they must now recognize their commitment to radical change and build an organization
opposed to the ruling forces which is free of their support. They
will withdraw applications for government support and distribute, through the present Central Council, all government
money given to them as individual centers. They also believe
that existing research efforts must be coordinated in order to use
previous experience for future planning. The format of the INFO
will therefore be changed. The undersigned centers agree that
they must eliminate all antiproletarian and nonpolitical aspects
of their activity. The centers must work with political groups
to organize cadres and to plan politically relevant activities.

The undersigned centers, finally, believe that the Central
Council must try to prevent liberal sabotage of the common task.
The Central Council must either serve work groups or be dissolved.

This resolution is only a suggestion. We shall discuss in our
work conference on May 17 whether it can actually serve as
a basis for action.

When the centers no longer needed to present a united front
to the Senate in order to get money, political differences finally

became clear. The liberal groups insisted on the original principles of the centers and thought work with their own children sufficient political activity. They did not want to see that the centers, unless altered, could not possibly attain their major goals. Experience had already shown that the centers could only be educational models for a very limited and privileged academic class. This was particularly clear with regard to our principle of getting people to organize in small groups to do educational and political work.

It was also obvious that we had not achieved one of our original aims, the liberation of women through the centers, much less that dream of liberating women from other social groups by involving them in such work. The women had discovered that the amount of work required in most of the centers left them no time or energy for other commitments. Admittedly, many began to understand their own needs and to make concrete efforts to get out of coercive family situations. However, this did not amount to a fulfillment of our political goal. The women, therefore, concluded that they could not achieve even a limited emancipation within the capitalist system by battling men, but only by struggling outside the centers against the class society in alliance with men.

In confrontations during this period, the liberals' chief argument was that the "socialists" had given no serious thought to the content of the new education, and that they only wanted to use the children for political purposes. Therefore, said the liberals, it was absolutely necessary to draw up a clear and detailed program for education, to consider toys and books and, at long last, to begin working on preschool education as originally planned.

The radicals insisted, with reason, that so far the politically active individuals in the centers had always been the ones to bring up constructive ideas in the discussions (e.g., sex education, the role of the teacher, significance of collective play, historical prototypes, etc.). Their next argument was more important: only when it was clear who this education was going to serve would it make sense to thoroughly go into the matter of educational content. It had become apparent that no model of liberation would automatically, or by means of propaganda, spread to other population groups.

The liberals simply would not face the fact that the factors which prevent such centers from spreading through the population concern class: lack of money, time, and educational experience. Workers cannot use nonauthoritarian education as we know it now, because it cannot be reconciled with the circumstances of their lives, which are still marked by miserable living conditions, lack of facilities for children's play, the parents' perpetual fatigue because of their exploitation at work, and their obsession with filling their leisure hours with the culture of substitute gratification foisted on the public by an economy geared to consumption. From the point of view of time and physical and psychological resources, intensive concern with children is virtually impossible. Right now, nonrepressive experiments are a luxury which only the privileged — academics, independent professionals, and middle class individuals — can afford.

The radical members countered the argument that they were avoiding the concrete task of education by pointing out that they were only refusing to continue to give a better education to their own children in their own privileged class while doing nothing to help the masses. They proposed instead to evaluate their work in education politically and to connect it with recent activities in the movement, specifically by collaboration with workers' organizations, building school-connected centers in working class neighborhoods, and working with kindergarten teachers.

Because of these discussions the Central Council was reorganized into three task forces. Participation in one was mandatory for members of the Council. One group met with a task force of kindergarten teachers and social workers to organize a strike by West Berlin kindergarten teachers. The second studied children's organizations run by the German worker's movement between the two World Wars, intending to use this knowledge in the battle which the plan to set up school-connected centers would probably provoke. The third group was to coordinate work done by the centers and various workers' groups, on the organizational level as well as in action, and to turn the Central Council into a "Center for Sexual Politics."

The Day Care Centers Council issued a leaflet discussing their job:

The Left has finally begun to realize that organizational changes are needed. As everyone knows, the belief in working with the proletarian masses, based on the need to act with fundamental economic groupings, has won general acceptance in the movement now. The organization of revolutionary cadres will be based on economic groupings.

Most Day Care Centers agree that they must now cooperate with the cadres and help in any activity which will further their goals.

The Central Council, therefore, cannot continue to coordinate a child raising service for the bourgeois. It will do just that, however, as long as it creates study groups to amass theories verified only by our own petit bourgeois projects. We run the risk of basing rules for socialist child raising on our limited experience, having no knowledge of the worker's life except the indirect and dubious findings of "social class research."

We shall try, using our experience and the help of politically conscious men and women in workers' organizations, to formulate a new revolutionary theory. The Center for Sexual Politics in the Grunewaldstrasse will serve as an educational center for workers' groups, open to all members of those groups.

The Center will provide the kind of education which will be of immediate value to members of workers' organizations.

In contrast to orthodox education, this training will teach cultural revolution; it will erase the artificial separation of work and leisure and will show that the laws of sexual repression and those of production are identical. Finally, we must understand that, objectively, scholarship serves the ruling class and we must question it!

The three groups survived for about two months. The first dissolved when the West Berlin kindergarten teachers' strike failed. Something of the same nature happened to the other groups. Many people from politically diverse centers were extremely interested in the program and the meetings were crowded; however, the original members of the groups did all the actual political work. The center of action, therefore, shifted from the Central Council to workers' groups — that is, groups trying to set up centers for proletarian children.

The liberals in the Council's work groups confined themselves to the role of critical consumer. So the political members decided to stop working under the auspices of the Central Council and to use other quarters for their meetings. This meant, in effect, the end of the Central Council of Socialist Day Care Centers. Significantly enough, the liberal Day Care Centers, which were in the majority, made no attempt to organize politically.

New Political Outlook for Preschool Education

The political groups which made up the former Central Council are still active, but they are now organizing among West Berlin workers, not working in Day Care Centers. They resemble only slightly the former centers in their activities, social composition, principles, and political outlook. The members are no longer primarily interested in the education of their own children. The nonauthoritarian movement is transforming itself into a socialist organization in which educational concerns are subordinated to political ones.

Before we explain briefly the philosophy and actions involved in the new trend, we must make one observation. We have learned that the Storefront Centers and the educational and political theories upon which they are founded can be understood by anyone who makes a serious attempt. However, the political framework which shapes current work in socialist education is no longer comprehensible to the mentality of liberals, left wing critics, or even "socialists" who work in isolation. For one cannot expect intellectuals to be sympathetic towards methods of fighting and organization in which their theoretical perspective, however radical they think it may be, must be dissolved on the grounds that, objectively, it serves capitalism as long as it is not directed to organizing the proletariat. We decided to leave the nonauthoritarian student movement mainly because of what we learned outside child raising projects and outside the universities.

In the light of our new orientation and insights, two groups with different political viewpoints on the matter of education have emerged. We shall describe briefly the groups and their ideas.

ROTKOL

The Red Educational Collective (ROTKOL), formed by some people who originally staffed Schöneberg 2, spent months in Kreuzberg with several social workers and teachers, getting practical experience. They combined the center children and children of neighborhood workers in a large center with a playground. The Collective published the results in "Goals and Methods of Proletarian Education" (March 1970).

The Left must now work out a revolutionary strategy, based on adequate analysis of social classes and the problems of organization, which can be applied on a national scale. It must also take the first steps toward developing a socialist program on a national scale. This will be possible only if the movement has its roots in the proletariat, in the neighborhoods, and in the economic situation of the workers.

There are several reasons for the importance of work with proletarian youth:

1. Young workers are less integrated into capitalism. Therefore they do not feel as strongly as their parents the need to identify with either anticommunism or the revisionist policies of the KPD (German Communist Party).

2. In the last few decades, capitalism has tailored a substitute culture for working class youth. The content itself— encouraging the authoritarian family, repression of sexuality, insistence on a male and female mystique — proves the collapse of bourgeois ideology, for those old foundations are buckling now. "Hippies and the counter-culture, the spread of drugs as a means to individual liberation, and increasing time in school are creating, even for the working class, the type of adolescence which permits identification with certain liberties and which will make it harder to accept the discipline of work in adult life." The reaction set off by these signs of a relaxation in the general mood of repression took the form of anticrime campaigns and stepping up public youth programs, which can only "make working class youth and everyone else more conscious of repression and manipulation."

3. "Antiquated and authoritarian schools overwhelm working class youth with antiproletarian, antisexual and depoliticizing lies, which repress and modify some of their energies to transform them into greedy consumers."

4. Vocational "training" has become meaningless and falls below standards required for technical work. Students are widely used as cheap labor, are heavily exploited by industry, and are generally forced to do piecework.

5. Working class youth, as numerous incidents go to snow, lack the inhibitions of university students in fighting their oppressors, for they have not internalized as fully the morality which holds private property to be sacrosanct.

The history of the working class movement shows that re-volutionary proletarian youth have a major role in revolutionizing the entire working class, especially in the phase of stimulating and organizing class conflict. Children and youth have been reached, however, in the Federal Republic and West Berlin, and some working class youth are now ready to join militant youth organizations.

The book summarized the situation now:

If socialism today is to anchor itself in the proletariat, it can best begin with proletarian children and youth. We must intervene in the educational and child raising process, which has reached a state of crisis, and stop that process from instilling passive adaptation to capitalism. Since working class youth today are socialized not only in the school, factory, and family, but class in the leisure time youth culture specific to the working class, it is necessary to formulate strategies of struggle, research, and education for that area. Strategies must consider each neighborhood as an individual case in order to utilize the potential for agitation and mobilization among proletarian youth. Problems of house, family, and marriage, leisure for the worker; the connection between damage done by the production system and the kinds of consumption supposed to serve as a remedy; the high pressure of piecework, the problem of the embourgeoisement and depoliticization of the working class — all these problems can be articulated to suit the age group and the neighborhood and used to determine specific methods of organization. From here, the changing consciousness of the proletarian masses can generate further concrete stages in organization, class analysis, and programs.

Before work in a neighborhood can really proceed, three conditions must be met:

1. Research must be done on the relationship between family, school, and street, in order to assess class structure and the potential for militancy in a particular sector. One could use official statistics, questionnaires, or experimental actions.

2. ROTKOL members must be thoroughly trained. They must study all relevant texts, including documents on the history and philosophy of Communist education movements in the twenties and the connection between theory and practice as explained in Marxist-Lennist classics and in Mao Tse-Tung.

3. Cooperation with other socialist groups to avoid doing

"projects." ROTKOL thought it particularly important to work
with groups active in proletarian education in West Berlin.

PROZ-ML

The second political viewpoint was held by PROZ-ML (the
Proletariat Women's Center of Marxist-Leninists in West Berlin)
— a group of parents, active in the original Day Care Centers,
and working women who started a center in a working class
neighborhood. Unlike ROTKOL, they did not see their work as
revolutionary activity, with a general political strategy adapted
to the needs of the socialist movement.

Criticism of previous work in the centers began with this
point:

At that time, the solution of child raising problems and of the
sexual entanglements experienced by parents seemed a necessary
preliminary for revolution. Revolution was our goal, but we forgot an absolutely essential step — the organization of the
proletariat (RPK, #36, 24.10.69).

There was one major criticism of cooperation with workers'
groups undertaken by PROZ-ML. We believed that workers,
too, should enjoy the advantages of nonauthoritarian education
in the centers. We believed it would be difficult to transfer the
model of the centers to working class children, however, because the workers were far more authoritarian with their children
than we were even before we founded our centers. But we
thought the transition would be eased if we linked the nonauthoritarian Day Care Centers with workers' organizations.
We believed that, through discussions of authoritarian education,
workers would probably better understand their oppression
at work.

Collective education can only be effective if parents deliberately
analyze the way they previously raised their children. This can
only be achieved by making the connection between oppressive
experiences at work and a repressive family atmosphere
(KL-INFO 7).

We learned that working class women were, in fact, fully

aware of their double oppression; but they were resigned because they couldn't imagine how a Day Care Center or a workers' organization could really help. For this reason, we gave up the plan of developing Day Care Centers connected to places of work. The attempt to politicize the workers around problems of child raising and to organize them around this task, therefore, had to be given up.

How can we organize working women, and around what issue? Wherever there are working women and wherever our agitation and propaganda reach them, any issue is favorable. Agitation and propaganda must be used to stimulate proletarian women to educate and organize themselves. Organization begins with education.

Agitation and propaganda must be grounded in our own knowledge. Our own education must begin in an organized way.

The dialectic which we have suggested — agitation and propaganda leading to awareness through education and then to organization — presupposes centralization. It is essential that we centralize our political work.

Some jobs immediately suggest themselves: education, agitation, and propaganda in places of work and in workers' neighborhoods in order to get workers to organize on the principle of democratic centralism — an aim that has immediate consequences for practical work. This is the point where PROZ-ML differed radically from ROTKOL, which was trying to organize the proletariat locally in independent units, with no clear plan for getting the different groups to "cooperate (!) to produce a revolutionary mass organization." In addition, the various groups in PROZ-ML follow a comprehensive educational program, which is continually reexamined to ensure that it remains valid.

"Working women's desire for a basic education, provoked by our agitation and propaganda, will be a first step to organization." The basic education follows four principles:

1. An understanding of the basic contradiction in capitalism is essential to achieving a proletarian consciousness.
2. We must establish a dictatorship of the proletariat by destroying the bourgeois state.
3. Dialectical thinking is the method of the proletarian struggle and the education of the masses to socialist class consciousness.

4. Revisionism must be fought, and that fight is the test of the first three principles. We must have a Communist critique of the revisionist parties (including the German Communist Party and SEW). Second, we must study the history of the working class movement to learn from its triumphs and successes. Third, we must study the history of the working women's movement; we must analyze the glorious international struggle of women in oppressed nations; and we must study matriarchal societies.

Politically aware proletarian women will need a kindergarten for their children. This kindergarten will be the beginning of a children's collective which, however, will not be run primarily by the working mothers themselves. . . . This kindergarten will not be specifically connected with an economic enterprise . . . it will be a Children's Home and will generate manifold other organizations such as further Homes, Storefront Schools, etc.

We have described nonauthoritarian education and the development of the West Berlin Day Care Centers in their historical and political context. That story is another proof of what we said in the introduction, that education is intrinsically related to the whole of society — in short, that we will win the fight against repressive education only if we manage to destroy the capitalist state apparatus and its educational system. Success, however, depends on building a nationwide proletarian organization to fight for the economic, political, and social interests of the people. One sentence can sum up the lesson of the Storefront Day Care Center Movement: if you really want a kind of child raising worthy of human beings, in which the needs, capacities, and interests of all children can be fostered and fulfilled, you must work for the larger political goal.

This does not mean that members of the movement should raise their children in a repressive way or even send them to public kindergartens. It means that we no longer think that the nonauthoritarian education of our own children is, in itself, revolutionary work.

We are convinced that working in preschool education within a proletarian mass organization can again be highly significant as a practical help and a mobilizing factor, especially for women. What we learned, in experience and theory, in the Day Care Center Movement, will not go to waste. The idea of replacing authoritarian family structures by political collectives of adults and children, however, will have revolutionary potential only when it is applied to a militant working class.

Only then shall we see what use can be made of nonrepressive principles such as group decisions on sexual life, resolution of conflicts by the group, and concrete actions of solidarity and resistance. What we know about nonauthoritarian education of petit bourgeois children definitely cannot be transferred unchanged to workers' children. For their class generates basically different forms of socialization. To define these differences and to draw practical conclusions for organizing proletarian children and youth will only be possible in the context of the new kind of action. At this point, all we can do is speculate.

If you want direct knowledge of a thing or a complex of things, you must join the actual struggle to change reality, participate in the effort to change the thing or complex of things; only in this way can you make contact with the appearance of those things, and only by personal participation in the actual struggle to change reality is it possible to distinguish its essence, or the essence of the complex of things, and to understand it. . . . If you want to learn, you must take part in an activity that transforms reality. If you want to know the taste of a pear, you must transform it; that is, you must put it in your mouth and chew it. If you want to know the structure and properties of atoms, you must conduct experiments in physics and chemistry to change the nature of the atom. If you want to know the theory and methods of revolution, you must join the revolution.

— Mao Tse-Tung, "On Practice," *Selected Works*, Vol. I, p. 353

Index